The Cuban Revolution

A Captivating Guide to the Armed Revolt That Changed the Course of Cuba, Including Stories of Leaders Such as Fidel Castro, Chè Guevara, and Fulgencio Batista

Free Bonus from Captivating History (Available for a Limited time)

Hi History Lovers!

Now you have a chance to join our exclusive history list so you can get your first history ebook for free as well as discounts and a potential to get more history books for free! Simply visit the link below to join.

Captivatinghistory.com/ebook

Also, make sure to follow us on:

Twitter: @Captivhistory

Facebook: Captivating History:@captivatinghistory

Contents

A revolution is a struggle to the death between the future and the past.

- Fidel Castro

Introduction

The story of the Cuban Revolution is the story of an effort that should never have succeeded.

Cuba had only just gained its independence when the country found itself in a brutal tug-of-war between dictator after dictator. The Americans that had been so intensely involved in liberating it from the grasp of the Spanish quickly began to exploit it using the Platt Amendment; even after the amendment was abrogated, Cuban presidents arose and seized power in coup after bloody coup. But none of these would be worse than Fulgencio Batista, a man who would be responsible for the deaths of tens of thousands of people.

Yet this is not so much the story of the revolution as it is the story of the three inimitable men behind it: Fulgencio Batista, Fidel Castro, and Ernesto "Chè" Guevara. Each of these controversial figures have a gripping story behind their actions, and this book aims to explore their lives and how their backstories brought them to their roles in the revolution.

The first two chapters of this book will provide a brief overview to the history of Cuba, giving depth and understanding to how the revolution came to be. After that, it will plunge into the lives of Batista, Castro, and Guevara, and tell the tale of the revolution. It is a gripping story, the story of an impossible victory by a disadvantaged underdog who should never have won. It's a story about courage in the face of certain failure and utter determination against incredible odds. And ultimately, it is a story about perseverance, about hope and courage, about never giving up. It's the story of the Cuban Revolution, and it is an incredible adventure.

Chapter 1 – A Jewel in the Spanish Crown

The story of the Cuban Revolution is a continuation of the story of Cuba's struggle for true independence, a struggle that began as early as the fifteenth century. Power after power rose up and attempted to take control over Cuba, and it was only with the revolution that the island truly stood alone for the first time.

Or perhaps that statement is a little inaccurate. There was a time, hundreds of years ago, before Christopher Columbus, before the Spanish, before all of this, that Cuba was truly independent—an island that belonged to no one except its own people. This was the time of the Taíno.

People of the Free Cuba

The first people to populate Cuba moved there from South America sometime in the eleventh century. These, the Guanahatabey, were a primitive tribe of hunter-gatherers who lived primarily on shellfish and lived in peaceful little groups along the seashore. Not much is known about these people; they kept to themselves, taking little from the island's resources and leaving little in the way of a footprint behind. Time has since erased almost every trace of their existence.

About two hundred years after the Guanahatabey traveled to Cuba, they were followed by a more advanced group of Arawak Indians—

the Taíno. These were farmers as well as hunters and had a more complicated society, as well as a complex mythology. The Taíno were the first people to ever play with a rubber ball or to smoke a cigar. Tobacco was one of their most important crops, as well as yuca, a kind of potato-like tuber that could be harvested and processed into flour, which was used to make cassava bread—still a staple in many areas of Africa and Latin America today.

The Ciboney were a similar tribe of people who populated western Cuba; these were a subgroup of the Taíno people, but a little less advanced than the Classic Taíno who inhabited the eastern and central parts of the island.

The Taíno were a peace-loving people, although they made war on the neighboring Carib tribes, who came from the mainland of South America. They did coexist fairly peacefully with the Guanahatabey. It was unsurprising, then, that they received European explorers with open arms, little knowing that the arrival of the explorers heralded the end of their peaceful lives.

First Contact with Europeans

When Christopher Columbus landed on the shores of Cuba on October 28th, 1492, he thought it was India.

The Spanish explorer had left the coast of Spain two months earlier with three ships and a band of nervous sailors, heading west into the apparent void on a quest to establish a new trade route to Asia. He was certain that there had to be an easier way to get to Asia than sailing all the way around Africa; surely, considering that it was now common knowledge that the earth was round, if you sailed far enough the other way you would eventually end up on the other side of the world. It was an ambitious idea at the time, and it would have worked perfectly but for one small problem: America was in the way.

When the explorers arrived, Columbus was convinced that Hispaniola—the first land they sighted—was an island off the coast of Asia; Cuba, he thought, was a peninsula of the mainland itself.

They were met by a group of friendly, dark-skinned people whom Columbus immediately referred to as Indians, a name that still sticks to Native Americans today.

The Taíno welcomed the Spanish explorers with joy. They believed that these light-skinned people had to be servants of their god of light, Yucajú, and treated them with hospitality and respect. They brought the explorers treasures from their world—corn and yuca and tobacco—to exchange for bits of glass and other little trinkets. But there were two things about the Taíno that really got Columbus' attention. The first was their gentleness and friendliness; traits that, he wrote to the Spanish king and queen, would make them good "servants." The second was their gold. Both men and women had golden necklaces and earrings sparkling against their skin, and Columbus knew he had just stumbled upon a literal goldmine.

The Conquest of Cuba

Columbus left a small settlement in the New World before sailing back to Spain, his ships laden with new treasures from the Americas, including a few Taíno. Delighted with his discovery, the Spanish Crown sent him back on a second voyage the next year, along with a command to be friendly to the natives and establish a good relationship with them. It was a command that Columbus and his men would wholeheartedly ignore.

The Spanish sailing to the New World changed from explorers to conquistadors (Spanish for "conquerors"), and instead of befriending the Taíno and other natives, they proceeded to exploit and attack them. It is not too dramatic to say that the Spanish wiped out the Taíno as an entire civilization. When the conquistadors first arrived in the 1490s, there were twenty-nine Taíno chieftains ruling over 350,000 Cubans; by 1550, there were less than five hundred Taíno left.

The conquest really began in 1514, led by Diego Velázquez, who would later become the first governor of Cuba. This conquest decimated the Taíno. Those who resisted were slaughtered; those who did not were harshly enslaved and worked to death. Women were raped or forced into marriages with Spanish sailors. The most devastating killer of all was disease. Smallpox and other illnesses that came with the Spanish from Europe were completely alien to Taíno immune systems, and it killed them in the thousands.

By the mid-sixteenth century, the Taíno were all but gone. Sebastian de Ocampo had circumnavigated the island and it had been established as a Spanish colony of the New World. The Indians were not Indians after all, but it mattered little now because most of them were dead. Only a handful remained, and they were eventually given a little land and some rights under the Spanish New Laws passed to protect the natives in 1542.

Cuba officially belonged to Spain. And it would continue to do so for more than three hundred years.

Spanish Cuba

At first, when it had just been conquered, Spain paid little attention to Cuba. The Spanish Crown was more interested in gold, silver, and other precious metals; these were more abundantly present in Hispaniola, Brazil, and Peru than in Cuba itself. However, it quickly became evident that Cuba had one great natural treasure that would facilitate trade between the Old and New Worlds for centuries: Havana Bay.

Havana was one of the first settlements to be established on the island, and it remains the most important city today. The natural bay made a perfect rest stop for trade ships on their way back to Europe with American treasures. The settlement also provided them with practical necessities to get them across the vast ocean, items like food, wood, and water. As more and more trade began to occur between the Americas and Europe, Havana rose in importance until it became the compulsory stop where all Spanish merchant vessels would come together before their journey home in the famous Spanish Treasure Fleet.

Cuba would pay the price for its importance in the form of pirates, with important towns like Havana and Santiago de Cuba regularly being sacked and burned to the ground by marauding freebooters. However, it recovered from each blow, and by the eighteenth century, Havana was a heavily fortified city known as the Key to the New World.

The island itself also quickly proved to be a lucrative asset for Spain. Tobacco was one of its first important exports, but its importance was quickly dwarfed by one of the most luxurious and expensive food items of the time: sugar. Cuba's climate was perfect for the cultivation of sugar, and it became a major item for export to the Old World. In fact, after the Haitian Revolution in 1791, Cuba became the leading sugar producer in the world.

Sugar caused Cuba's economy to boom, but it had a dark and bloody side that has left a permanent scar on history: slavery.

Cuban Slavery

As early as the mid-sixteenth century, it became evident that Cuba was running out of labor. The Taíno were dying out, and employing Spaniards was expensive, so plantation owners turned to the cheapest workforce available: African slaves.

The first slaver arrived in Cuba in 1526, carrying a cargo of men and women who—only months ago—had been living normal, free lives, with homes and families, jobs and businesses. Now they were nothing but merchandise. Many of them had already died on the brutal voyage across the Atlantic; some starved, some succumbed to the European diseases for which they had no immunity, and some flung themselves into the sea, considering bondage to be worse than death. Those that had survived were heartbroken and sickly, and now they were about to enter the horrors of a life in which they had no rights, no choices, and no voice.

Over more than three hundred years, Cuba would rest much of its sugar industry on the scarred and beaten shoulders of the sugar slaves. These slaves endured an intolerable existence. They were whipped, starved, raped, and mistreated in every way imaginable; they worked 20-hour days on pitiful rations, and if they slowed down, they were beaten.

The appalling conditions that sugar slaves had to endure can be summarized with a single number: eight. This was the number of years a slave—even a young adult, the most commonly traded age— could be expected to stay alive once they started working on a sugar plantation.

Spanish Tyranny

The Spanish, who had treated the Taíno so poorly, did not improve their actions as the centuries slipped by. Decade after decade, they continued to exploit both native Cubans and African slaves, and even after Great Britain and the United States abolished slavery, the Spanish were still importing hundreds of thousands of slaves into Cuba. At the peak of the slave trade, one-third of the island's population consisted of enslaved people.

It was not only the slaves that were being abused by Spanish oppressors, however. Cuban-born people—often of mixed race— found themselves struggling on one of the most prosperous islands in the New World. While the economy flourished, about 90% of the profits were going to Spaniards, who only made up 8% of the population. Discontent grew among the Cuban population; they knew that they were being exploited, and many Cubans supported abolition, yet Spain stubbornly clung to the slave trade. In the early nineteenth century, small uprisings started to take place throughout the island, primarily in the eastern Oriente Province where most of the sugar plantations were located. These were rapidly crushed, and Spanish methods of punishing those who dared to revolt—and of trying to extract information from suspects—grew more and more brutal.

By 1868, Spanish tyranny had become unbearable, and a Cuban lawyer and plantation owner by the name of Carlos Manuel de Céspedes decided that something had to be done. An organized rebellion had to rise up, greater in numbers and smarter in strategy than the scattered attempts at revolts that had taken place beforehand. This time, slave and slave owner would have to stand together to achieve anything.

The Struggle for Independence Begins

On October 10th, 1868, Céspedes walked up the steps of his sugar mill, just like he did every morning. And just like he did every morning, he rang the slave bell to summon the slaves for work. But unlike every morning, today he took out a sheet of paper and some nails and attached the paper to the door of the mill. Then he turned to his slaves, and he told them that they were all free.

Céspedes had written the 10th of October Manifesto, a manifesto for the rebellion that he and some other key players had been working on together over the past few weeks. He and fifteen others had signed it. The manifesto spoke of independence from Spain, racial equality, and the abolition of the slave trade. "Our aim is to throw off the Spanish yoke," it said, "and to establish a free and independent nation."

It was an ambitious idea. Just how ambitious became evident as war waged for the next decade, earning this failed fight for independence the name of the Ten Years' War. In Cuba, it is known as the Great War. Spain pulled out all the stops, employing brutal executions—often of innocents—and other cruel tactics in an attempt to destroy the handful of fierce rebels rising out of the Oriente Province.

The war was drawn-out and determined, but ultimately, the rebels just didn't have the resources to win. After the government of the Cuban Republic in Arms fell apart—leading to the deposition of Céspedes and, eventually, his death—the rebel effort went steadily downhill. By 1878, the war was over. Some slaves had been freed, but there was no abolition, no independence, and no rebel victory.

Spain could relax—for now. The fight had only just begun.

Chapter 2 – America Gets Involved

For almost four hundred years, Cuba had belonged to Spain—a country more than four thousand miles away. Yet it was also close neighbors with one of the greatest powers in the world: the United States.

Florida is only ninety miles from the Cuban coastline, and the U. S. had long been capitalizing on the riches of its tiny neighbor. Many Americans owned businesses or even lived on the island, and trade relations were good. Newspapers, politicians, and the American public watched Cuba's fight for freedom with interest. Having only abolished slavery more than twenty years after the United States took that step, Spain was already seen as something of an enemy in the eyes of the average American; and the tragic heroism of the Cuban rebels had started to capture the public imagination.

The fight for independence did not end with the Ten Years' War. In fact, it was only beginning.

The Little War and the Abolition of Slavery

In August 1879, just a year after the end of the Ten Years' War, trouble brewed in the Oriente once more. Major General Calixto

Garcia, a veteran of the Ten Years' War, wasn't done with fighting Spain yet. Having been one of the few rebel leaders that refused to sign a pact with Spain at the end of the war, he had fled to New York after the war and immediately started working on a new rebellion there. War was declared on August 26th, 1879. The ensuing struggle was demoralizing and utterly fruitless. The island's morale and resources had been so depleted by a decade of fighting that the latest rebellion was doomed before it even began. It ended in September 1880 with utter defeat, becoming known as the Little War (La Guerra Chiquita).

Stunned into silence by repeated defeat, the Cubans continued to labor under the oppression of their Spanish occupants. The people felt trapped, incapable of rising up, having seen the terrible aftermath of the two wars the island had just survived. It was peacefully—and under pressure from Great Britain and the United States, not from the Cubans—that Spain finally abolished slavery in 1880, albeit implementing *patronato*: a system of indentured servitude that forced the "freed" slaves to spend the next eight years working for their masters at no cost. Considering the life expectancy of the average sugar slave, this was longer than most of them could still hope to live. However, the Spanish Crown finally abolished both slavery and *patronato* entirely in 1886.

Slavery was gone; racial equality was still only a distant hope. Literate whites outnumbered literate blacks three to one. Afro-Cubans were banned from certain seats in public spaces and from certain jobs or even whole professions. Cuba was also no closer to independence, as Spain was determined to cling stubbornly to its island.

Yet although there was no further attempt at an uprising for fifteen years during the so-called "Rewarding Truce," Cubans had not let go of their dream of freedom. In particular, there was a young man hiding out in Mexico who had not given up on independence. He was a stirring poet and a passionate leader by the name of José

Martí, and he was the spark that would ignite a firestorm the Spanish could not contain.

The Cuban War of Independence

José Martí was only fifteen years old when the Ten Years' War broke out, but his imagination—and then his convictions—were quickly captured by the rebel cause. His parents were Spanish immigrants; his heart was wholly Cuban. In 1869, at the age of sixteen, his passionate writings in support of the rebels landed him in prison for the first time. Far from deterring Martí, imprisonment only served to make him even more determined to free his country of the chains with which he found himself now bound.

Martí fled Cuba just before the end of the Ten Years' War, spending time in other areas of Latin America and finally landing in New York. It was here that he began to plan another bid for freedom, a plan that would finally start taking shape in 1894. Aided by military men Máximo Gómez and Antonio Maceo (the general who had clung on tenaciously at the end of the Ten Years' War, refusing to capitulate for months against overwhelming odds), Martí started the insurrection on February 24th, 1895. He presented the Manifesto de Montecristi, which outlined the rebel plan for victory. The key element of the manifesto was participation by all blacks: a not inconsiderable feature, bearing in mind that black and mulatto (mixed race) people made up the majority of the Cuban population at the time.

Another important feature of the new war—one which had been neglected in the Ten Years' War—was the destruction of businesses and assets that supported Spanish loyalists. While private Spanish landowners who did not oppose the insurrection were largely left alone, loyalists' cane fields were set on fire in a bid to level the playing field in terms of resources.

The Cuban Republic in Arms was brought back to life, and the fight began once again in the Oriente Province, heading toward the western provinces—including Havana—which the rebels knew they would have to capture if they were to have any hope of success. And as the war began, hope of success grew. The seventeen-year Rewarding Truce had allowed tension and passion to simmer among the people once more, and they rose up in strength and numbers that the Spanish had not anticipated.

In response, Spain sent more than two hundred thousand troops to Cuba, led by General Valeriano "The Butcher" Weyler. Weyler began to employ the most brutal tactics he could think of in an attempt to crush the growing rebellion. Likely the worst of these was the concentration camps, the implementation of which was known as the Reconcentration Policy. Spanish soldiers swept through the Cuban countryside, driving ordinary farming families from their land and forcing them into horrific camps in the cities. Livestock was destroyed and crops abandoned; those in the camps had no way to feed themselves and were hardly fed at all. To add to this problem, the soldiers were fresh out of Europe and carrying those same diseases that had wiped out the Taíno. Disease spread through the camps, killing those that the Spanish did not. It is estimated that Weyler's tactics killed as much as twenty-five percent of the Cuban population.

Appalling and drastic as Weyler's tactics were, they were also doomed to failure. Although Martí was killed just a few months after arriving in Cuba, the insurrection continued to gain strength. Reconcentration only served to infuriate the ordinary Cubans, making them flee to the arms of the rebels in support of their cause. The rebellion gained momentum and started to sweep farther and farther westward. By the end of 1897, Spain recognized that it was not going to beat the rebels into submission. Instead, it attempted to pacify them. Weyler was replaced, and a new government was implemented in Havana with more lenient policies toward the Cubans.

It wasn't enough for the rebels. For them, this time it was independence or nothing.

Yellow Journalism in the United States

American newspapers had been printing articles about the Cuban War of Independence since its beginning, and the *New York World* and *New York Journal* were in fierce competition to sell the most papers. William Randolph Hearst of the *Journal* and Joseph Pulitzer of the *World* were determined to make money and sell newspapers by any means, and it quickly became evident that the war in Cuba was the hottest story around. Cuba was an underdog that looked like it might be winning, and Americans loved an underdog. Independence and freedom were also—then as now—near and dear to the American psyche, and so the two papers set about turning the war into a narrative that their readers wanted. Like any narrative, it needed an atrocious bad guy that the readers would love to hate, and Spain was the perfect target.

Spain did indeed treat the Cubans with cruelty during the war, but perhaps not quite as much as the newspapers led America to believe. In a practice known as "yellow journalism," writers started to exaggerate or even fabricate stories about Spanish brutality to tempt their readers into buying more papers. The Cuban effort was portrayed as that of a struggling, impoverished nation that was bravely fighting but couldn't hope to win on its own. It didn't take long for these tactics to drive the American public into pushing for war. The United States was thirty years out of the Civil War and had been presenting a united front for those decades of peace; it was hungry to prove itself in war with someone other than itself.

President William McKinley, however, was not as keen on war as his people were. For a start, he had seen action himself in the Civil War and knew that it was not as romantic as some of the public would have liked to believe. Apart from that, McKinley couldn't declare war on a nation that was still one of the major European powers just because his people liked the idea.

But in February 1898, events in Havana Bay would force McKinley's hand. The U. S. S. *Maine* was about to explode.

Remember the *Maine*

In late January 1898, Spanish loyalists in Havana broke into an uncontrollable riot. Newspapers in Havana had started to publish scathing articles about the Spanish army's horrific treatment of native Cubans, and loyalists protested by burning down several printing presses. Worried for the safety of American citizens in Havana, the United States responded by sending one of their warships, the majestic U. S. S. *Maine*, to lie at anchor in Havana Bay. The ship's mere presence was more than enough of a deterrent to keep the Spanish from causing harm to any Americans, and its several hundred soldiers found themselves enjoying something of a holiday.

Until the night of February 15th, 1898. Most of the men were asleep when, suddenly and without warning, the *Maine* exploded. A fireball engulfed the ship, instantly killing many soldiers; despite rescue efforts, many more burned to death or drowned as the blazing ship sank to the bottom of the bay.

The explosion was a lit match to the petrol-soaked American public. 260 Americans were dead, and they all unanimously blamed the Spanish. When an American investigation revealed that the *Maine* had been blown up by a mine, presumably Spanish, it was the last straw. President McKinley declared war in April 1898, and the United States marched on Spain in the Philippines, Puerto Rico, and Cuba itself.

The Spanish-American War

By this point, the rebels had already pushed Spain almost to the breaking point. Contrary to what the average American had been led to believe, the rebels were not only winning— they had almost already won. Spain was clinging on to Cuba by its fingernails; its resources were finally feeling the strain of decades of war throughout its borders and colonies, and when the mighty United States brought its advanced weaponry and vast numbers into the fight, Spain knew it had been defeated before the war even began.

The Spanish-American War lasted only until July 17th, 1898—less than three months from start to finish. The American victory was brisk, decisive, and cost only a handful of casualties. Cuban rebels welcomed the assistance and guidance of their massive neighbor joyfully, not only in procuring the victory, but in establishing the island as an independent country.

While the United States annexed Puerto Rico and established a governor over Cuba, it was promised that as soon as the island was ready, it would be given independence. Preparations began to draw up a constitution, establish a new government from the battle-worn remnants of the Cuban Republic in Arms, and hold the first general elections for the newly-freed nation.

In December 1901, the election took place—the beginning of Cuba's brief democracy. Tomás Estrada Palma, one of the politicians that had also been involved in garnering U. S. assistance during the war, was elected the first president of Cuba. The next year, with the government firmly established, the United States withdrew its occupation of the island. Cuba was independent at last.

But its democracy would not last for long. A line of dictators was standing ready to exploit the people yet again. And arguably the worst of them all had just been born in Banes, Cuba, to two poverty-stricken people who could never have known that their son was going to grow up into the terror of Cuba.

The Birth of Batista

It's possible that no dictator has ever had a less likely start than Fulgencio Batista. His life changed entirely from his birth to the time when he took power—less like turning over a new leaf, though, and more like uprooting an entire forest. In fact, when he was born, he wasn't even called Batista yet.

Born on a farm twenty miles outside of Banes, he was the son of an ex-rebel army sergeant named Belisario Batista Palermo and his mistress, Carmela Zaldívar. Belisario Batista was not married to Carmela, and when his son was born, he refused to even allow the child to be registered with his surname. Carmela was left to name, register, and raise him on her own. She called him Rubén Zaldívar, giving him her last name because his father did not want him.

Young Rubén was a mulatto, and his DNA bore testimony to almost every race of people that had contributed to Cuba's mixed history. There was Taíno blood in there, the blood of the peaceful "Indians" who had welcomed the Spanish and then been slaughtered by them. There was some Spanish, too, that race that had discovered this jewel of the Caribbean and connected it with the rest of the world. Then there was some African, the influence of slaves who had been dragged across the Middle Passage in the most horrendous conditions in order to labor on the cane fields to produce an opulent luxury for the lazy rich. There was even some Chinese blood in him, a result of the indentured workers who had been shipped to Cuba from China (ironically, considering that Columbus had originally thought that Cuba *was* a peninsula of China) to replace the emancipated slaves. He was a melting pot of different races, an illegitimate child, and a member of an impoverished family, and therefore rejected not only by his father but by a society still reeling from the blows of war.

But one thing was for certain. Rubén Zaldívar was all Cuban. And while, for now, he was just an unhappy child in a poor community, he was going to grow up into a man that would change the course of Cuban history. Forever.

Chapter 3 – Becoming Sergeant Batista

Postcard of a railroad station in Santa Clara, circa 1900

Little Rubén was only seven years old, but already he was no stranger to work. He'd only been about four or five years old when he'd started assisting his mother in her work on the fields as an agricultural laborer. But now, his mother had decided to relocate herself and her illegitimate little boy to the town of Banes, moving away from the countryside. She hoped that she could find better work as a maid or a cleaner and that Rubén would be able to go to school, getting the education that she likely never had under the Spanish regime.

As Rubén and his mother traveled through the countryside and into Banes, they probably spotted a few American soldiers along the road. Even though the U. S. soldiers had originally withdrawn in 1902, Cuba was once again crawling with American military. Independence had turned out not to be as easy as it looked. Tomás Estrada Palma's first term had been controversial but peaceful. He had improved infrastructure across the island, started to restore a country that had been ravaged by decades of war, and improved education, too—one of the only reasons that a poor child like Rubén could hope to get an education at all. But many criticized his relations with the United States. For a start, he had been elected president only when his single opponent withdrew, complaining that the U. S. was showing favoritism toward Palma. Palma had followed this up by agreeing with the Platt Amendment, which gave the U. S. pretty much free rein to do almost anything they liked to Cuba. For a start, it permanently leased Guantanamo Bay to America for a naval base. And, more crucially, it also gave the U. S. the right to intervene militarily to protect American interests on the island.

In 1906, this is exactly what happened. The second ever Cuban presidential election in September 1905 was rigged. Palma and his associates wanted to ensure that he would stay in power for the next term. This time, his opponent was not as easily cowed; José Miguel Gómez, the leader of the Liberal Party, had been a leader in the Cuban War of Independence, and he was not going to be pushed aside by a mere politician like Palma. He was also popular among the people, who saw him as a hero of the war that had set them free from Spain's iron grip. When it became evident that Gómez was likely to win the election, Palma's Conservative Party rigged it. Gómez lost, but he and his followers knew exactly what had happened.

At first, it appeared as though Palma would be allowed to serve his illegal second term in peace. But in August 1906, the Liberals rose up in a violent revolt that threatened to overthrow the government completely. Both government and revolutionaries turned to the United States, clamoring for assistance. Palma believed that the U. S. would be his ally because of his implementation of the Platt Amendment; Gómez appealed to the American ideal of free and fair elections, wanting Cuba's powerful neighbor to supervise the elections to keep them from being rigged again.

President Theodore Roosevelt, whose Rough Riders had been part of the American force that gained Cuba's independence in the first place only a few years before, was initially reluctant to assist either side. However, he consented to send William H. Taft—then the secretary of war—to Cuba to assess the situation.

On September 28th, 1906, two things became obvious: the Americans were going to have to intervene, and Palma was not going to gain any support from them. Knowing that he had no hope of beating a combined force of Americans and Liberals, Palma resigned. America invaded a few days later, arriving on October 6th, 1906, and the Liberals—who wisely recognized that this was a good sign for their cause—immediately surrendered. One week later, Charles Edward Magoon was made the provisional governor of Cuba.

Known as the Cuban Pacification, this military action was almost entirely nonviolent. Strict discipline was imposed and obedience to the current government demanded, but there was little real resistance. Instead, the Americans turned their attention to building roads and keeping the Cubans as placid as possible, reminding them that putting a foot out of place would be an unwise move in the face of the power of the United States.

By May 25th, 1908, Magoon was confident that the situation in Cuba was stable enough to hold a round of elections. The United States closely supervised these, and of course, Gómez was elected president later that year. In February 1909, the last of the U. S. troops were pulled out.

Rubén had little awareness for such things, however. He just hung on to his mother's hand as they made their way through the town, looking for a better life for them both. Perhaps he stared up at the American soldiers in their shiny uniforms and thought how they represented everything he didn't have: power, importance, a full belly every night. It's possible that his encounters with these splendid soldiers—so captivating to the imagination of a seven-year-old boy—served as the inspiration that, years later, would lead him to the Cuban army.

For now, Rubén started attending a public school in Banes. His mother went to work as a maid in the house of the Diaz-Balart family, and Rubén proved to be a good student, soon being given a scholarship to night classes at a Quaker School of Friends. This was run by American missionaries, who started to teach young Rubén to speak and write English. Soon, he had developed a reputation for reading anything he could get his hands on.

Rubén was eleven years old when Cuba once again found itself in an uproar. Gómez's term had come to an end, and with the 1912 elections on the horizon, the Partido Independiente de Color—an Afro-Cuban political party—redoubled its efforts to win the election. They were formed in 1908, the year that Gómez was elected president, and had spent the past four years gaining power. While slavery had long since been abolished, Afro-Cubans still found themselves continually coming second to their fellow white citizens. Despite the fact that black Cubans had made up three-quarters of the liberation army that had set Cuba free, the PIC argued that Afro-

Cubans were not being recognized for their efforts in the War of Independence. They did not have the same opportunities as whites, and the idea of white supremacy was still prevalent.

With the majority of Cubans still being black, the Liberal Party that was in power at the time under Gómez knew that if the PIC really gained power, it could become the ruling party in Cuba. Trying to suppress the movement, a Liberal senator passed an amendment that banned any party that was formed based on race, regardless of what race that may be. PIC leaders did not heed this new amendment, and they were promptly arrested and the PIC officially disbanded.

But the members of the PIC weren't done yet. On May 20th, 1912—the year of the next presidential election—they rose up in an armed revolt. The revolt was led by Evaristo Estenoz, who was well experienced in rebellions. He had been a lieutenant in the War of Independence and a general in the 1906 uprising; now he found himself rising up against the very liberals whose cause he had once advanced. Despite being jailed in 1910 and the official dissolution of his party, Estenoz rallied his men and began an armed demonstration that struck terror into the Cuban government. Cuban troops were deployed to hold off the attack, and the United States was approached for help. Uncle Sam, at the time, was still deep in its period of racial segregation; the idea of a black person running for president was alien to this nation, and so on May 25th, the first American troops were sent to Cuba to assist in crushing the rebellion.

Lasting a little more than a month, the rebellion was bloodily and cruelly crushed. Despite hard fighting from the PIC, they were outnumbered and quickly gunned down. Estenoz himself was killed on June 27th, after which the movement lost momentum. 2,500 American troopers were deployed, and about 5,000 Afro-Cubans were massacred. The PIC was not only out of the presidential election—its members were almost all killed.

In the November 1912 elections, Mario García Menocal—leader of the Conservative Party—was elected president. Relative peace was restored across the island. But for young Rubén Zaldívar, the entire world was about to end.

Still despised and rejected by his father, Rubén's one true ally was his mother, Carmela Zaldívar. She was his champion and provider, despite the fact that she was only fifteen years old when Rubén was born. It was to her that he turned for love and care, and even though she had three other boys to raise, her relationship with Rubén was integral to his childhood. Poor as he was, at least he had Carmela. She was his closest friend; her nickname for him, "Beno," bore testimony to her fondness and affection.

But he wouldn't have her for much longer. In 1915, three years into Menocal's term, disaster struck. Carmela Zaldívar died. Rubén was only fourteen, and with his mother gone and his father as distant as always, he felt truly alone in the world. His father immediately moved the four boys—most of them illegitimate—out of Banes and onto the sugar plantation where he worked as a cane cutter. As the oldest boy, Rubén had no choice but to abandon his studies and go to work on the cane fields with his father. This did not last long; within a few months, he turned to bookkeeping and weighing cane in the office, while the other boys were sent to live with friends and relatives while his father continued to work on the plantation. But the gaping hole Carmela had left in Rubén's life could not be replaced by any amount of work. He wanted to get away. He *needed* to get away, and when he was fifteen years old, that was exactly what he did, hiking westward from Banes into an uncertain future.

Meanwhile, Menocal ran for president again in the 1916 elections. The election was rigged; political violence erupted across the country, and fifty people died before Menocal was elected once more. While Cuba experienced an economic boom, the country's morale was still nosediving. After the high of gaining independence, the people struggled with corrupt leaders for more than a decade, and Menocal was no exception. Nepotism was one of his particular specialties, and even though Cuba was gaining riches, its people were dissatisfied.

None more so than Gómez, still the leader of the Liberal Party. In February 1917, he staged yet another armed revolt against the conservative government. Chaos broke loose across the island, centered on the eastern provinces of Camagüey, Santa Clara, and Oriente. Once again, both rebels and government appealed to the United States for help. The U. S. was embroiled in the First World War, with many troops already fighting in Europe, but a few troops were spared to go to Cuba in support of the government. The short-lived rebellion was over by mid-April, with five hundred people dead. Another round of elections was held that same month, and Menocal was reelected. This time, nobody dared oppose him, and he held onto control of the island.

Rubén was still in the eastern provinces of Cuba at the time, mostly in Oriente, but he had little awareness of the growing rebellion. He had more pressing matters to attend to—the necessities of survival. His first stop after leaving Banes was the home of his maternal aunt, Candida Zaldívar, who lived on an orange farm. Rubén went to work helping to pick and package the oranges, but he quickly found that staying there was unbearable. Candida spoke of Carmela all the time and even referred to him as "Beno" just like his mother had. But she wasn't his mother. His mother was gone, and he didn't know where to run to get away from that truth. Abandoning the orange farm, Rubén briefly went back to Banes just as the rebellion was breaking out in Santa Clara. But his father still hated him and his mother was still dead. Within a few weeks, Rubén was wandering off once more. He left behind his home, his family, and even his first name. He couldn't bear for anyone to call him Beno ever again, so he abandoned his first name of Rubén and started introducing himself to strangers by his second name: Fulgencio.

This time, he decided to walk away from the agricultural industry that had supported his family for years. Instead, he turned his attention to a new prospect: the railroad. An American tycoon had established this new railroad from Havana to the eastern provinces not long before, replacing a trade route that had formerly been traveled almost exclusively by horse carriages and oxcarts. The train was faster, stronger, and never got tired, and so hundreds flocked to work on it. Better yet, labor there was unionized; railroad workers had rights that agricultural laborers could only dream of. To Fulgencio, who was homeless at the time, this sounded like an incredible prospect.

He spent weeks hanging around railroad stations, sleeping in whatever nook he could find, playing dice for food, and trying to find *somebody* from the railway who would just take a chance on him. He managed to persuade a conductor to give him a lift to Antilla, a port town on the east coast, hidden away in the caboose. It was here that Fulgencio would come face to face with his country's tumultuous politics for the first time. Spanish immigrant railroad workers were engaging in a violent strike against the United Fruit Company. The company was looking for Cubans to replace these stubborn Spanish, but Fulgencio refused to accept the job, choosing to join the strike instead.

For years, he continued to bounce from railroad to agriculture according to where he could find his next meal. His dream was the railroad, but he found himself harvesting sugarcane and oranges more than once. It felt like a breakthrough when, in late 1918, he finally found permanent employment on the railroad and began to travel all over the island. At first being employed as a brakeman, Fulgencio worked his way up to trainee conductor. It was while performing this job that he fell from a moving train and almost died; his right leg was horribly wounded, and he was out of work for weeks, lying in a hospital in Camagüey as he recovered. At one point, it looked as though the leg would even have to be amputated, but the doctors managed to save it, although he bore an ugly purple scar on that limb for the rest of his life.

Once he had recovered, Fulgencio returned to work on the railroad, but not for long. Change was on the horizon. The railroad workers were continuing to strike and protest; Fulgencio did not take part in most of these, but it did mean that employment in the industry was haphazard and plagued by violence. His work on the railroad had provided Fulgencio with independence; still, he wanted to improve his situation and his education as much as possible. It was time for a change, and when Fulgencio considered his options, he remembered those uniformed soldiers he had seen in Banes when he was only a child. They had inspired him then, and more critically, they were better paid now.

Fulgencio's mind was made up. He was going to join the army. In 1921, he bought a railway ticket to Havana and enjoyed the train as a passenger instead of a laborer for once. Alfredo Zayas was president of Cuba, having been elected in one of Cuba's very few peaceful elections, which had been closely supervised by the United States to prevent another disaster. The island was more or less at peace, but there was always room for more in the army since unrest was never far from the surface. Fulgencio had no difficulty signing up once he reached Havana.

It was more than just a new job to the young man, however. Now twenty years old, he was still not fully healed from the agony of losing Carmela, but he was proud of what he had achieved. In only five years, he had gone from a homeless and destitute teenager to a self-made, independent, and fairly successful young person, someone who could do anything he wanted with his life. He wanted to leave his ugly past behind and start something new, something powerful, something prosperous. That meant he had to leave his identity of Rubén Zaldívar—the illegitimate mulatto child, the mongrel boy without a mother, the kid that nobody really wanted—behind forever.

When they asked him his name, he told them it was Fulgencio Batista.

Chapter 4 – The Sergeants' Revolt

Havana was an entirely new world for Fulgencio. Having grown up in the countryside of the eastern provinces, he was awed by the bustle of Cuba's capital city. Stationed at Camp Colombia, he stayed in the barracks just outside the city, but he was still able to experience its chaos and beauty.

Cuba's current leader, Alfredo Zayas, was a poet and a thinker, unlike the military men who had been president before him. Zayas was a profoundly intellectual man who aimed for peace and tranquility. Still, corruption was not unheard of in his government, although it was considerably less corrupt than the administration immediately before and after him. He was faced with what appeared to be insurmountable odds when he was first elected in 1921: when sugar prices spectacularly nosedived after World War I, Cuba found itself bankrupt. Although Zayas' solution—a fifty-million-dollar loan from the United States—may have been somewhat questionable, it was certainly effective. He was able to improve on education, freedom of speech, and communication, establishing Cuba's first radio station in October 1922.

Tourism was also flourishing in Havana at the time, with Americans flocking to this tropical paradise right on their doorstep. Times were peaceful, even good; as a result, Fulgencio did not see any action during his first two years with the army. Instead, he was taught typing and stenography (shorthand). Shorthand was a vital skill at that time, since this was before recorders were in use, and a fast and accurate stenographer was a valuable asset. The skills also appealed to Fulgencio's literary tendencies and he quickly established himself as one of the best stenographers in the area.

In 1923, Fulgencio decided to return to the eastern provinces for a while, working as a supervisor on a sugar plantation there for a few months. He returned to Oriente a very different person than the half-orphaned boy who had so disconsolately trekked off to join the railroad years before. Then, he had been an utterly destitute, grieving fourteen-year-old son of a cane cutter; now, he was twenty-two years old, fully independent, and working as the overseer of men doing the same work his father had always done when he was a child. Fulgencio felt that he had finally made it. But this was just the beginning of his successes.

It wasn't long before Fulgencio returned to the army. And it was also around this time that Zayas' peaceful presidency came to an end, and the first Cuban dictator rose to power: Gerardo Machado.

The youngest general of the Cuban War of Independence, Machado had been only twenty-seven years old when the United States occupation of Cuba began. Although it's said that he and his father had been cattle rustlers before the war—something that cannot be proved due to a suspicious fire that destroyed criminal records in the area—Machado began a successful political career during the occupation, starting by being mayor of Santa Clara. He became president in 1924 after winning the election against ex-president Menocal.

At first, things looked promising under Machado. While still protecting trade with the United States, he was more devoted to the idea of Cuba as an independent country than his predecessor had been. His presidency saw the construction of a seven-hundred-mile highway, among other things. Meanwhile, Fulgencio had returned to the army and was making a name for himself as a top-class young stenographer.

1928 was the year that young Fulgencio was officially commended as the fastest stenographer in the entire army. He was promoted to the rank of sergeant first class at Camp Colombia, just one step below the rank of officer, even though he was still a relatively young man—just twenty-seven. It was also the year that Machado's presidency took a turn for the worse that ended up becoming a dictatorship. Throughout his presidency, Machado's attitude toward any opposition had become increasingly dictatorial, a fact that was only worsened in the public imagination when he changed the constitution to allow himself a six-year term. He employed violence and bribery to push all other presidential candidates out of the November 1928 elections so that he would be sure to win them.

The people were already dissatisfied when worldwide economic disaster struck: Wall Street crashed in 1929. Cuban sugar prices, which Zayas had just managed to nurse back to health, fell dramatically. Open protests, some of them violent, started to erupt across the country, and Machado did not help matters by creating a secret police—the "Porra"—to squash these uprisings using any means necessary.

The stage was set for a revolt that would oust one dictator, but in the same breath, turn a successful young sergeant into an even worse leader. Yet at the same time, the seeds of Cuba's last revolution were being planted: one in Oriente, and another in Argentina.

Fidel Castro was born on August 13th, 1926. His early childhood eerily echoed that of Fulgencio Batista. Also born in the eastern provinces, and also illegitimately, little Fidel was also raised on a sugar plantation. His father Ángel Castro y Árgiz, a Spanish-born plantation owner, had fought on the Spanish side during the War of

Independence; now, however, he was all Cuban. Fidel was his third child to Lina Ruz González, a Canarian woman who worked in his household and became his mistress even though she was nearly thirty years younger than Fidel's father. Despite the fact that Ángel Castro was thoroughly wealthy at this point, Fidel spent his early years among the farm workers' children and became accustomed to poverty.

Fidel was two years old, and Fulgencio had just been made a sergeant when the third key player of the Cuban Revolution was born in Rosario, Argentina, on June 14th, 1928, to two black sheep of their respective families: the rebellious feminist Celia de la Serna and free spirit Ernesto Guevara Lynch. They had only been married for six months when Celia gave birth to their first child, a little boy to whom they gave his father's name, Ernesto.

Both Fidel Castro and Ernesto Guevara were still just toddlers when Machado's dictatorship reached its cruel extreme. Machado was arresting his opposition and putting them through unfair trials that only ever ended with imprisonment or execution—even for the innocent. Public outrage was spreading rapidly throughout the island as Machado's brutality only continued to increase. The police and army were struggling to maintain control over a country that was increasingly unhappy and had spent so many years staging revolutions that violence seemed to be the only answer. By the beginning of 1933, Cuba had the look of an island at war. Not wanting to engage in yet another deployment of thousands of U. S. troops to this pesky island, President Franklin D. Roosevelt sent diplomat Sumner Welles to sort out the Cuban situation. Handsome Harvard graduate Welles tried his best to reinstate the constitutional guarantees that Machado had suspended in order to further his own interests, but Machado wouldn't budge, and Welles had no choice but to remove him from presidency in an attempt to keep the peace.

The attempt failed. Even though Machado was removed from government, the people were still raw from the recent savagery.

They wanted a revolt—and a revolt they would have, with Fulgencio Batista at its head.

Fulgencio was thirty-two years old when Machado was removed and a new provisional government was installed. The provisional president was Carlos Manuel de Céspedes y Quesada, the son of that original Céspedes that had first rung his slave bell to call his country to arms for independence. Welles hoped that Céspedes would be able to govern the country for the remainder of Machado's term, allowing Cuba to reorganize itself into something capable of democracy, but it was not to be. The president may have been replaced, but most of his crooked cronies were either allowed to peacefully leave the country without trial or—even worse—left in their positions. In particular, the army was filled with Machado's officers, men who were still set in the ways of cruelty and oppression.

Machado fled the island in August 1933, recognizing that there was no regaining control now. Céspedes was made president on August 12th and would rule for a little less than a month. While he did bring the 1901 constitution back and took steps toward eliminating corruption, it just wasn't good enough for the people, particularly not the common soldiers. They were still being ordered around by the same people, officers that they didn't trust and didn't agree with. Worse, those fair and just officers that had been removed by the corrupt Machado regime were not reinstated. Other issues like backpay and lack of promotions for good soldiers that weren't friends of Machado were fuel to the fire. The soldiers' anger only grew as they saw that their supposed allies, the U. S., had failed to set them free. It was time to take things into their own hands once more. Arguably, this action was rather premature considering that Céspedes had only just started trying to put together a country that had been torn apart by years of corrupt government and then by a paralyzing general strike.

As the best stenographer in the army, Fulgencio had been the one to record the many corrupt and twisted trials. He had been witness to so many of the unjust sentences, seen so many innocent people dragged away to a life behind bars or even to death. It angered him, and it also opened his eyes to how it had angered the rest of the men. Perhaps at that point Fulgencio saw the opportunity that had presented itself. He was hungry for more authority and power than the rank of sergeant could give him. He never again wanted to be that child that nobody wanted, and he was about to show the world what he could do.

On August 19th, 1933, he attended the funeral of a fellow sergeant that had been killed by Machado, and it was the opportunity he needed to speak out. In his speech that day, Fulgencio delivered rousing, emotive words that captured the imaginations of the enlisted men. He may not have seen action, but he was one of them—a familiar face that they knew and trusted, and his words captivated them. It was time to stand against this corrupt regime, Fulgencio told them. It was time to make a change for enlisted men and, although they didn't know it yet, for the entire country.

Fulgencio and a group of others—mostly lower-ranking military men and some civilians, including a journalist, who served to keep Fulgencio in touch with the civilian world—started to hold meetings throughout various venues in Havana. They told their superiors that these meetings were merely to plan how to make life better and easier for their fellow soldiers, but actually, they were planning to overthrow their officers.

By the end of August, preparations for the coup were complete. On September 1st, a devastating hurricane struck the eastern provinces of Cuba, causing terrible damage and immediately drawing President Céspedes' attention away from the brewing political situation. He left Havana for Santa Clara to survey the damage and arrange support and repair work for the ruined provinces, providing Fulgencio and his men with the perfect opportunity to stage the coup they'd been planning for weeks. Fulgencio called a meeting of soldiers and sergeants at Camp Colombia on September 4th, planning to use the meeting to finalize the last details of their strategy for improving conditions for the common man in the army. However, before the meeting, some of the officers got wind of what was about to occur. Instead of trying to suppress the coup, they nominated a young man—a Captain Mario Torres-Menier—to attend the meeting and hear what the men had to say about their grievances.

The sergeants and other soldiers were considerably surprised when Torres-Menier showed up at the meeting, but they allowed him in anyway and immediately bombarded him with demands. Rumors had been going around that there were going to be pay cuts and that people were going to be retrenched, and it made everyone nervous. The soldiers started to accuse Torres-Menier of ignoring their requests; he was bewildered not only by the sheer number of men that attended the gathering, but also by the vehemence with which they presented their complaints.

Finally, Fulgencio rose up and presented a loftier speech. He spoke about the rights not only of the soldiers, but of every citizen in Cuba, and expressed his readiness to make sacrifices for the entire nation. Although none of the men—much less Torres-Menier—appreciated the scope of his speech, it was a foreshadowing of what was to come, a hint at what Fulgencio was really planning. It was never really about simply improving conditions for soldiers. The revolt that Fulgencio actually wanted to lead was against the entire government. He was determined to prove that he was more than his past, more than just the best typist in the army, more than a mere sergeant first class. Fulgencio Batista wanted power, and he was ready to seize it with everything he had.

Torres-Menier eventually left the meeting with his tail between his legs, promising to present the men's grievances to the rest of the officers if they would give him a formal list of complaints. They did not believe him—or, at least, they did not believe him once Batista had told them that they shouldn't. The sergeants were supposed to call a meeting that same afternoon to draw up the formal list, but the list was never presented to the officers. Instead, Batista spent the day contacting other allies in Havana and the Matanzas Province, gathering his troops for battle. He was not after a peaceful resolution—he was after war.

At about eight o' clock that evening, Batista called a massive meeting of sergeants and enlisted men in the movie theater of Camp Colombia and told them that the officers had ignored their requests. There was no way they were going to get what they wanted by such peaceful means, he told them. They would have to turn to action.

"From this moment forward," Batista told them, "do not obey anyone's orders but mine."

Thoroughly riled up by their charismatic leader, the men unanimously agreed. As one, they turned against their officers and rushed through the camp, taking control over it. The officers had no control over the men; vastly outnumbered, they offered no resistance to the sergeants.

News of the sergeants' success in taking the camp spread rapidly throughout Havana, and others who had decided to stand against the Céspedes government—especially the Student Directory—hurried to the camp to support the sergeants. The Student Directory in particular quickly recognized the importance of the victory. Their leaders discussed the possibility of riding the momentum of the revolt beyond the military and into the city, planning to overthrow the entire government. Batista didn't take much convincing; it's possible that this had been his aim all along. He agreed, and together with the students, they sat down that very night to write a new political manifesto and put together a government for their growing revolt.

By the morning of September 5th, the revolt was being presided over by a government of five men called the Pentarchy. These men were lawyers, faculty members of the University of Havana, and one journalist; Batista was not one of them, but it rapidly became obvious that they all actually answered to him rather than the other way around. In only a few days, the Pentarchy was dissolved and one of its members became the president of Cuba: a professor of the

University of Havana named Ramón Grau San Martín. Batista was made head of the Cuban armed forces, and thus began his career as a powerful politician.

Grau's presidency did not last long. His administration had a significantly radical, nationalist flavor that the United States immediately rejected, and Batista recognized that Cuba still needed Uncle Sam's help to boost its economy and give it somewhere to send its sugar. Pressure from Batista and the U. S. forced Grau to resign in January 1934, and he was replaced by the United Nations' Carlos Mendieta, which effectively fixed U. S. and Cuban relations.

For the next six years, president after president would rise and fall, none lasting very long, none making much of an impact, and every one of them effectively a puppet—and it was Fulgencio Batista that held the strings. He had had a taste of power, and in the space of a few brief months, he had changed from the army's best stenographer to the man who controlled the entire army. Having seen what chaos a revolt in the Cuban army could cause, it was evident that whoever controlled the army actually controlled the country. Grateful for the improvements that Batista had made for enlisted men—paying them better and being quicker with promotions—the army lent him unwavering support, regardless of who was president of the country.

It was only in 1940, after another military rebellion, that Batista would finally be elected president of Cuba. But the real transformation had taken place during that fateful revolt of 1933. He became a hero of the people then, establishing himself as a man who had the potential to control a nation. They were encouraged by the many improvements that were made after the revolt; for example, women could vote for the first time, minimum wage was increased, and the Platt Amendment that granted so many of Cuba's treasures to the United States was abrogated.

And so it was that in 1940, in a free and fair election, Cuba elected Fulgencio Batista as president. It would be years before the island realized the extent of its mistake.

Chapter 5 – Revolution Brews

Batista in Washington, D. C., in 1938

https://commons.wikimedia.org/wiki/File:BatistaDC1938.jpg

As Batista became the first non-white president of Cuba, the island found itself in a time of improving economy, yet increasing corruption. Batista's first term was relatively peaceful, even beneficial to the Cuban people. His adoption of the 1940 constitution was welcomed by the people as it aimed to improve living conditions for many Cubans by raising minimum wage, improving access to healthcare for everyone, and even removing capital punishment.

The constitution did not allow Batista to run for a second term, and he made no attempt to oppose it. In 1944, having served a peaceful term as president, Batista stepped down with no fuss at all. His successor—whom he had chosen himself and groomed for president for some time—was Carlos Zayas, a quiet, bespectacled lawyer whom Batista seemed to have chosen more for his willingness to do as he was told than for anything else. Perhaps the public recognized this, because Zayas resoundingly lost the election. Instead, Ramón Grau San Martín was reelected.

All this did not go unnoticed by a young man who had just enrolled in the University of Havana: Fidel Castro. Then nineteen years old, young Fidel had spent his childhood bouncing from one Catholic school to the next. Unlike the young Batista, Fidel was not much of an academic as a small child; he specialized in terrorizing his Jesuit teachers and generally running amok, paying much more attention to sports than school.

Still, Fidel's father was determined that something should be made of the boy. He encouraged Fidel to attend university, and the young man enrolled to study law at the University of Havana in 1945. Immediately he was plunged into the complicated world of Cuban student politics. UH students had been instrumental in the Sergeants' Revolt, and had long been a source of political revolution and change; so much so that corrupt Cuban presidents in the past had gone to dramatic extents to prevent student involvement in stirring up the people, such as temporarily closing the university.

Poor as the common man—especially those in rural areas—was at that time, Havana was a center of opulence and luxury, as well as corruption. The Havana of the 1940s was a playground for the very rich, which, at that time, mostly consisted of American movie stars and those involved in organized crime. In fact, the infamous Havana Conference—a meeting of mob bosses from all over the world, particularly America—was held there in 1946. People as notorious as Meyer Lansky and Lucky Luciano built hotels and casinos in Havana, where they were serenaded by the likes of Frank Sinatra. But where there was organized crime, there was also violence. Gangsters were shooting one another in the streets, prostitution and drug dealing were rife, and pimps were being killed on the street corners as gang wars ran amok throughout the city.

This *gangsterismo* culture soon seeped its way into the students of UH. For decades, students had been the most passionate protesters, always the first to oppose the government. Many leaders—including Machado and Grau—had turned to violence to suppress the students, having them terrorized by gangs with which the government was linked. This led to gangs being formed within the university itself. Many university groups were themselves involved in criminal activity, often committing violent acts. This was Fidel's first taste of politics and of war. And he found that he liked it. He began to join political university committees and to make a name for himself as a public speaker and a leader within the university, even beginning to carry a gun and go everywhere with armed friends when his life was threatened by other gangs in the university. But one thing that Fidel never got involved in was crime. He wasn't after power—he was after something more, a vision that he chased for the entirety of the Cuban people, for humanity as a whole. The poverty he witnessed in the rural areas where he'd grown up, and the corruption and violence he saw in the city that had become his home, was moving Fidel's dreams. He had once wanted nothing more than to become a major league baseball player. Now, throwing sports to the wind, he devoted himself to his studies of law, hoping to find some way of improving life for all Cubans.

Student politics were not enough for him. While he originally affiliated with multiple leftist student political groups, Fidel wanted something more; he wanted to be part of a real political party. In

1947, his mind was made up. He joined the Partido Ortodoxo—the Party of the Cuban People—which was led by Eduardo Chibás, a charismatic man who spent his entire life in politics. Fidel was attracted to Chibás' ideologies, which were against violence and corruption and called for a fair and free Cuba. He chose Chibás to be his political mentor and started to learn and grow under the older man while he continued his studies of law.

Meanwhile, in Buenos Aires, Argentina, the young Ernesto Guevara was himself beginning his university education. Like Fidel, Ernesto had spent most of his childhood playing sports, often encouraged by his doting parents. They had moved their entire family into the mountains of Argentina in the hope that the clearer air would ease Ernesto's asthma, a move that must have worked, as their son went on to become a successful high school athlete. He also showed an interest in politics from a young age, immersing himself in reading the works of William Faulkner, Karl Marx, and others.

In 1948, it was time for Ernesto to head off to college, and he chose to study medicine at Buenos Aires University. At the time, Argentina didn't look much different from Cuba. This nation, too, was reeling from the punches of the Great Depression; its struggling economy had led to unrest among the masses. In 1943, Juan Perón seized power in a military coup and ruled Argentina by decree. Under his rule, the economy was bolstered and education was made more freely available, but his iron-fisted grip on the country was reinforced by a brutal military that ruthlessly crushed any opposition. Like Fidel, Ernesto found himself discontented with this state of affairs. Even in his fairly privileged position as a medical student, he felt that the regime was oppressive, and he was determined to further explore the country and see what life was like for the rural communities.

Ernesto was still pondering a journey through the country when, in 1948, Grau's term as Cuban president came to an end. Elections were held once more, and an amiable man named Carlos Prío Socarrás was elected. Prío had been born in 1903 into an independent Cuba—

the first Cuban president born after the Spanish-American War—and had been involved in politics since his own time as a law student at UH. Like Grau, he attempted to improve some conditions in Cuba by arranging land reforms and building low-cost housing, but his rule was still marked by increasing corruption. Nothing was done about the gang violence that was destroying so many lives in Havana and elsewhere on the island.

Trouble was brewing throughout Latin America at the time as well, where the turbulent history of Cuba was being echoed in other countries and islands. A thousand miles from Cuba itself, on the South American mainland, Colombia was embroiled in decades of violence, and the situation there was about to reach a crisis point. In April 1948, Fidel and a friend found themselves in the middle of it when they visited Bogotá, the capital of Colombia. Their aim was to organize and participate in a Latin American Students' Congress, which was designed to counter the right-wing Pan American Conference that was being held in the city at the time.

Even though the twenty-one-year-old Fidel was used to the deaths of students and other citizens of Havana, he was shocked to discover the extent of the violence in Colombia. Back in Havana, he had taken part in protests over the death of a single student due to gang violence. Here in Bogotá, single deaths were going almost unnoticed. Massacres of thirty or more people were common: Colombians were dying like flies, and all for political reasons.

The Conservatives were in charge of the country at the time, but a Liberal leader had risen up and become a champion of the people. Jorge Eliécer Gaitán, the former mayor of Bogotá, was running for president, and the people loved him. His politics were questionable, but he was an undeniably brilliant orator and he had the charismatic ability to stir up a crowd. He spoke continually of how he was going to improve matters for the common man, and in a country that was well accustomed to corruption, his speeches were heady stuff. Critics called him a demagogue and a populist, but either way, the masses adored him. It was speculated that Gaitán was highly likely to win the upcoming presidential election.

Fidel was well aware of the election, but he was more focused on organizing his students' congress with his other associates. He did, however, get the chance to meet Gaitán, a handsome, clean-shaven man with sad, serious eyes. Fidel asked Gaitán to attend the students' congress, knowing that his presence would help the congress pack an extra punch. Even though he was busy with the election, Gaitán promised that he would come. He made an immediate impression on young Fidel, who was honored by Gaitán's promise to attend.

Both men went about their business—Gaitán to prepare for an upcoming court case in which he was serving as a lawyer; Fidel to distribute leaflets about various Latin American issues such as the dictatorship currently underway in the Dominican Republic and Puerto Rico's struggle for independence. This was perhaps an unwise move on the well-meaning young Fidel's part. The Conservative Colombian government of the time was quickly onto him, and he and his friend Rafael del Pino Siero found themselves promptly arrested. They spent some time being interrogated and kept in the cells, which only served to infuriate them and make them even more determined to hold the congress.

They never got the chance. When they were released on April 9th, 1948, the two boys stepped out into a scene of absolute carnage. The city was on fire, and the people had risen up in something that was not so much an organized revolution as it was a chaotic riot, a violent and desperate expression of their agony, rage, and dismay. It was called Bogotazo, and it was the single most violent riot during Colombia's most turbulent time, simply termed La Violencia (the violence). People were throwing stones and looting; they were setting public transport on fire and attacking public buildings, destroying them, pulling them down, and being shot at by the army and the police. There was smoke above them, blood on the street below them, flames and fury in the middle. The air was torn apart by noise—screams of anger and pain, gunshots, the brutal thuds of stones striking flesh, the sound of breaking glass. Bewildered, Fidel and Rafael headed toward Gaitán's office on the corner of 7th and 14th avenue for their next appointment with him.

They were still on their way when they heard the terrible news from people running in the streets: Gaitán was dead, killed just minutes ago. Emerging from a meeting with a group of sympathizers, he had stepped into the street and been shot in the chest at point-blank range by a lone gunman standing directly in front of him. There were rumors that this gunman had been a policeman, a pawn of the cruel government, and it drove the people mad, whipping them into a vengeful frenzy that extended across the entire city.

Fidel remembered the kind, intelligent man he'd met only days ago, and rage rose in him, rage against a government that would do this. Seizing a piece of an iron bar, he rose up and joined in the violence. It was his first taste of fighting on such an epic scale.

The Bogotazo would last for ten hours. In that time, about three thousand people died. Once the government had pushed them out of the center of the city and away from the government buildings, the people were more or less left alone to practically destroy downtown Bogotá. Molotov cocktails—petrol bombs made in glass bottles— were used to set buildings and vehicles on fire. Gaitán's suspected killer was caught and brutally murdered, his face bashed in with a brick, his mutilated body left in the streets. The young man would later be identified as Juan Roa Sierra, a possibly mentally ill person who had shown up at Gaitán's offices multiple times looking for work and been turned away one time too many.

The Conservatives had apparently not killed Gaitán; in fact, it's unclear exactly who did, as some witnesses claimed that Roa was not the killer after all. One conspiracy theory even implicated Fidel, although this is unlikely considering that Fidel had a good relationship with Gaitán and was in jail at the time of the murder. But the people would not be told this, nor would they have cared. They only stopped when the city was all on fire.

Sadly, Colombian violence did not end with the Bogotazo. In fact, this was just the beginning. In the decade to come, hundreds of thousands of Colombians would die in riots and revolts.

Fidel was unhurt in the riot. He and Rafael flew safely home to continue their studies, and in 1950, he graduated as a qualified attorney from the University of Havana. He was still a member of the Party of the Cuban People at the time and an avid follower of Eduardo Chibás, and it quickly became evident that his was no ordinary law practice. His aim was not to make money playing a corrupt system; instead, Fidel wanted to help the poor. He had grown up among the laborers on his parents' plantation and ever since then he had a heart for helping those so deeply locked in poverty. Seeing the rich politicians and the wealthy gangsters living it up in Havana had only further convinced him that something needed to be done for the ordinary people. As he worked with poor people in his law practice, Fidel started to find the capitalist model more and more abhorrent. It was in this time that he began to lean all the more toward communism in the hope that it would achieve a better life for the poor.

Four thousand miles away in Argentina, Ernesto Guevara was being similarly shaped into the revolutionary that he was about to become. In January 1950, Ernesto planned his first solo tour through Argentina. Wanting to see more of his country, he fitted an engine to his bicycle and drove his improvised motorbike all over the land—a route almost three thousand miles long that he tackled almost entirely alone. Two years later, he would take a second, much longer voyage, this time on a real motorbike named *La Ponderosa* (The Mighty). This voyage would take him through Argentina, Chile, Colombia, and Venezuela. But this was no ordinary tour. Ernesto didn't want to see glaciers or waterfalls; he wanted to see what life was really like for the ordinary people—particularly the poor—of Latin America.

What he saw appalled him. He visited the slums of the cities, the squalor of the leper colonies, and the belly of the Chilean copper mines, a place that he called a living hell. He encountered desperate beggars, an unemployed couple freezing to death in the Atacama Desert, and an old woman with tuberculosis who had been utterly failed by the public health system and was dying by inches in front of his eyes even as Ernesto tried to save her with the knowledge and the little equipment he had. He saw the dark underbelly of Latin America, and he saw that its tragedy was not violence: it was poverty. The real suffering did not only lie in gang violence and terrible riots. It lay in the eyes of the pot-bellied orphans who begged at the roadside, in the arthritic hands of old women trying to work to feed themselves no matter how sick they were, in the desperation for human contact of the lepers who were living without clothes or medicine in the ghastly leper colonies deep in the jungle. And it broke young Ernesto's heart. It was here, among the devastating poverty of the people, that the restless young medical student was formed into a revolutionary. Something had to change, and subconsciously, Ernesto began to blame the capitalist model for creating this terrible state of affairs.

In 1951, with both Fidel and Ernesto starting to form the same ideas—although they were still unaware of each other's existence—Carlos Prío Socarrás' presidency of Cuba was coming to an end. Cuba's economy was booming, but with every new pulse of prosperity that ran through the island, corruption was biting harder. Fulgencio Batista was the chief of Armed Forces at the time, but he was champing at the bit for presidency once more; his taste of rule in the early 1940s had not been enough for him. He wanted control, and he wanted it to last longer than a mere term. He felt that Cuba was rightfully his. And he wanted it back.

Still, even though Batista was a presidential candidate, he knew that he was unlikely to be elected. Far more promising a candidate was Fidel's mentor, Eduardo Chibás of the Party of the Cuban People. Chibás was telling the people about how he was going to clear out all of the corruption that was stifling the country, about how he would serve as a just and fair leader, cleansing the island of nepotism and violence. Unlike the other candidates, Chibás' words rang with authenticity, and he was expected to win the election.

A senator, congressman, and popular radio personality, Chibás was one of very few Cuban politicians of the time in whom history has never been able to find even a trace of corruption. He continually exposed corruption in other politicians, making him well liked by the people but intensely disliked by his fellow politicians.

On the 5th of August, 1951, Chibás was ready to make some more enemies. More specifically, he had been planning to expose the minister of education's embezzlement of vast amounts of government funds. Instead of building schools and helping children to improve their lives, this man had been feathering his own nest, and Chibás was onto him. At least, so he'd thought, and so he had promised to the people. But the congressmen who were meant to present evidence of the minister's embezzlement to him had utterly refused. They, too, were tainted with corruption, and Chibás, heartbroken, was forced to face the extent of the corruption that had eaten away at the entire government like rust. He could not deliver what he had promised; he despaired of ever turning Cuba into a country that was governed by fairness and truth, and he could see no way out.

So, instead of presenting the evidence he was supposed to have, Chibás used his weekly radio broadcast that day to warn the people of what was coming. Batista was going to overthrow the government in a coup, he warned; he had done it before with the Sergeants' Revolt, and he was going to do it again. Then Chibás said goodbye to his people, placed the muzzle of his gun against his abdomen, and fired off three shots. They tore his intestines apart. He was rushed to the hospital, where his body fought for life for almost two weeks, but his heart wasn't in it. He died on August 16th, 1951.

The 1952 elections were immediately in shambles. Chibás had been the man who was going to be president; now there was no real opposition, no real clear leader, and the people had no idea who to vote for with Chibás dead. While Chibás' suicide had been a devastating blow for Fidel and the people, for Batista, it was a stroke of wonderful luck. He did exactly what Chibás had warned that he would do. On March 10th, 1952, Batista headed to Camp Colombia—the place where he had become a sergeant and first put together the revolt that would end the Platt Amendment—and gathered together his men. The coup lasted less than an hour and a half. In the early hours of the morning, Batista's army took control of all the strategic points in Havana, killed two guards at the Presidential Palace, and unceremoniously removed Prío from his position as president. Prío and other members of his administration fled the country, and Batista canceled the elections and took what he believed to be his rightful place as the dictator of Cuba.

Rubén, the impoverished little boy whose mother was dead and whose father didn't want him, was dead as well. Even the intellectual young stenographer who had joined the army as Fulgencio was long gone. In their place stood Batista, a man who would stop at nothing to gain power. And power was what he now had.

Chapter 6 – MR-26-7

Moncada Barracks in 2013, commemorating the 60th anniversary of the attack

The death of Eduardo Chibás had flipped a switch in Fidel Castro. Chibás had been his inspiration, guide, even a father figure since Fidel's real father had always been distant. In the days and months after his death, even after Batista seized power, Fidel continued to visit Chibás' tomb with devoted regularity. "We will continue faithful to your ideals," he would tell his dead mentor, with tears in his eyes. "We swear we will complete your work, which we will never betray."

It soon became evident to Fidel that completing Chibás' work meant ousting Batista. The new dictator of Cuba became a symbol of everything that Fidel hated in an administration. Right after taking power, Batista swung hard toward the right wing; he cut ties with the Soviet Union and started to grow closer and closer to the United States. Even though he had been the one to abolish the Platt Amendment, Batista was now improving relations with the U. S., determined to grow Cuba's economy—and fill his own pockets— with American dollars. The fluctuating sugar price was no longer good enough to sustain the economy. Instead, Batista turned to tourism, but not the kind of tourism where families could gaze at natural wonders. He was building casinos and hotels, bars and clubs, turning Havana into a center of lucrative nightlife for gamblers and clubbers of every kind. Sectors like education, infrastructure, and healthcare suffered as Batista poured his focus into tourism. Fidel was forced to watch in horror and disgust as what he perceived as all the flaws of capitalism were laid bare before his eyes. As the poor grew ever poorer, the corrupt grew more corrupt and the rich grew richer.

Perhaps the greatest evidence for the extent of Batista's corruption is the solution he found for the violence and crooked casinos that were repelling American gamblers. Instead of enforcing the law or solving the issue of gang violence, Batista turned to Meyer Lansky, a prominent member of the Mafia. The two would form a tight friendship as the years went on; Lansky cleaned up the streets and the casinos, and Batista made him ridiculously rich. In fact, the rich of Havana were incredibly rich, but Fidel was not looking at them. He was looking at the poor people that came through his failing law practice every day.

Life was good, really good, for the rich people of Havana; in fact, even the vast middle class was doing very well. But the eastern provinces were suffering, perpetually and horribly. People were sick, people were unemployed, people were uneducated, and people were dying on the roadsides, waiting for transportation to come from somewhere and take them to clinics or hospitals in the cities. There was no glamour for those people. There was no fancy nightlife or gambling or luxurious hotels or white beaches. There was pain and hunger, and they were the people that Fidel saw.

Fidel was done with watching. He decided that Batista had to fall, but memories of the Bogotazo made him reluctant to resort to violence. Instead, Fidel began to attack the administration using the law in which he had been trained at UH. He brought lawsuits against various ministers and even Batista himself, accusing them all of crimes that were worthy of imprisonment. Fidel believed—and he very likely was right—that he had enough evidence to throw them all in jail, if only the justice system was actually just. But it wasn't. It was controlled by those same rich people who were benefiting so much from the tourism industry that Batista had built, and they had no intentions of overthrowing such a lucrative government. Every single one of Fidel's court cases failed.

By May 1952, it had become abundantly obvious that no legal means were ever going to be enough to take Batista down, not while the entire system was so obviously under his control. Somewhat reluctantly, Fidel was forced to turn to the one course of action that Cubans had been selecting over and over when their government failed them: violence. He started secret meetings in hidden apartments with other young people that were discontented with the administration—many of them fellow members of the Party of the Cuban People and followers of Eduardo Chibás—with a single goal in mind: planning the first attack of a revolt that was aimed to topple the giant that Batista had become.

Over the next year, Fidel slowly began to gather a tiny handful of rebels with enough spark and fire to stand against an army tens of thousands strong. There were not many of them, but their hearts were huge. Most of these were young people, often with little education and usually recruited from the ranks of the poor. Men and women, Afro-Cubans and whites and mulattos, they all had one thing in common: they wanted to beat Batista, and they were ready to follow Fidel into the jaws of death.

They were untrained and unarmed, but Fidel knew he could solve those problems. There was just one issue for which he did not have a solution: the fact that there was, at most, one hundred and sixty rebels in total. Their target, the Moncada Barracks in Santiago de Cuba, held more than ten times that number of Cuban army soldiers. These soldiers were all ferociously loyal to Batista and rigorously trained, so Fidel must have known that their attack had only the tiniest chance of succeeding. But he and his little army had to try. Disguising themselves as hunters or target shooters, they trained with their mismatched collection of firearms (some of which didn't always work), drilling until the motley crew of misfits had been turned into something resembling a fighting force. A young sympathizer who worked in a military hospital was recruited to steal uniforms out of the hospital so that the rebels would be kitted out like fellow soldiers, giving them the element of surprise in their attack on the barracks.

Fidel's aim was not so much to take the barracks as to raid them. He knew that their lack of weapons was a major flaw in their revolutionary plan; if they could just get into that vast armory at Moncada, they would stand a better chance of succeeding in their desperate battle. Gaining control over the communications in the barracks and using them to confuse the rest of the army could buy them just enough time to take the nearby radio station by force and broadcast some of Chibás' speeches to whip up the despondent masses into a country that was ready to rise up and overthrow its dictator. It was a wildly optimistic plan, one that could only possibly work if luck was entirely on their side, and even then the idea was still touch and go. But the idea was all that Fidel had, and he and his tiny band of half-trained, poorly equipped rebels would just have to try.

July 25th was the 100th anniversary of the birth of José Martí, the hero who had brought about Cuban independence, and the entire island was filled with celebration. Even though the people were once again being oppressed, at least, they reasoned, Cuba was still free. A grand festival was held, and its epicenter was Santiago de Cuba. It was the perfect cover for Fidel to gather his little army without suspicion. Piece by piece, in buses and cars, his army assembled on a farm in nearby Siboney, the rebels all pretending to be just ordinary young people wanting to celebrate the festival.

Nothing could be further from the truth. In the small hours of the morning, when the tropical heat of the summer sun was still just a hint on the edges of the still, dark air, the rebels gathered at the farm and were given their briefing. Fidel told them the plan, handed out their weapons and uniforms, and inspired them with one more speech. He split his little force into three groups: one to attack the military hospital, one to attack the Palace of Justice, and the third and largest group to go with him to the barracks themselves. Fidel's group would form a large convoy with most of the cars, hoping that the soldiers at the barracks—most of whom were still either drunk or sleeping after the evening's festivities—would mistake them for a routine group of soldiers accompanying one of Batista's cronies. At 4:00 a.m., the rebels left the farm and split off into their respective directions.

The groups heading toward the military hospital and the Palace of Justice—the latter led by Fidel's brother, Raul Castro—were made up of fairly seasoned men, some of whom had seen combat before. But Fidel's group, although it was the largest, consisted of the most inexperienced soldiers, and this turned out to be a mistake. Everything that could have gone wrong went wrong. Even before the rebels had reached the farm, some of the cars had gotten lost or developed flat tires; some of the rebels willing to join the fight even had to be left behind because there just weren't enough weapons for all of them.

Things did not improve once the rebels moved out from the farm. First, the convoy got separated; most crucially, though, the car carrying the rebels' heaviest weapons just disappeared into thin air. Reports differ on what exactly happened as the rebels approached Moncada Barracks. Some say that they happened upon an unexpected troop of soldiers, conducting a special patrol due to the festival; others say that Fidel lost control over his car, which was in the lead. Fidel himself claimed in his autobiography that he saw the guards at the gate of Moncada had realized that they were no ordinary convoy and that he crashed his car into the gate in order to incapacitate them as much as he could. Either way, Fidel's car ground to a halt against the gate in a heap of crumpled wreckage, and the guards immediately opened fire. The element of surprise that the rebels had so carefully planned for was utterly lost. The alarm was sounded with the rebels still outside the gates of the barracks, and the ninety rebels found themselves in a direct shoot-out with more than a thousand soldiers. With many of their weapons gone, Fidel's fighters didn't stand the slightest chance of winning the fight. In moments, many of the rebels were lying dead around Fidel's feet, and he was forced to call a retreat. Some of his men were captured; others, including Fidel, escaped into the countryside and hid.

Things were not going much better for the groups at the hospital and Palace of Justice. The rebels at the hospital were forced to flee, leaving eighteen of their number in the clutches of Batista's army. These battered rebels were then shipped briskly to Moncada, lined up inside the barracks' target range, and systematically killed. Knowing full well that what they'd just done was murder, the soldiers then dragged their bodies out toward the gates where the main battle had taken place and scattered them around to make it look like they'd been killed in combat.

These eighteen were only a portion of those murdered by the Batista regime in the next few days. Of the 135 rebels, only 99 survived.

Nine were killed in the battle itself; the others were captured, tortured for confessions, and then killed by a firing squad. Fidel and Raul, who had been hiding in the surrounding area, were captured only a few days after the failed attack. They had managed to hide themselves for only a short time, but it was time enough for the rest of the country to hear about what had happened. The details were sketchy, but one thing was clear: a brave and tiny band of rebels had attempted to dethrone the corrupt government by whom the people were being so oppressed, and the Cuban public rose in outrage, demanding that those captured be given fair trials. In a country where police brutality was rife and political opponents were being killed off like rats in a barrel, the people knew full well that the rebels were going to be executed, and their fury was such that Batista knew he was on the brink of witnessing a violent riot the likes of the Bogotazo if he simply executed Fidel Castro.

Instead, Batista tried to humor the people while still attending to his own agenda. Instead of putting Fidel, Raul, and the fifty-one other rebels that had been captured to the firing squad, Batista decided to make them stand a highly publicized trial. The trial was televised and almost everyone in Cuba found themselves tuning in to see what would become of the man who dared to stand against Fulgencio Batista.

The trials began on September 21st, 1953. Fidel and the other rebels had twenty-four attorneys at their disposal to help defend them, but Fidel refused to allow any of them to work with him; he trusted no one, and as a qualified lawyer himself, he asked to represent himself. His request was granted, and his first trial was a spirited attack on the Batista regime. Instead of trying to wriggle out of what he had done, Fidel argued that the Batista regime itself was what was at fault. All his research and work for the lawsuits he had brought against the government in the past year stood him in good stead now as he attacked the administration, defending his right as a citizen to rebel against what was illegal. The courtroom was stunned at his unconventional defense, but the public was inspired. Here was someone who was spitting in the face of failure, a man who remained fearlessly rebellious even once he had been captured and faced imprisonment or even death. Their imagination was captured even more when Fidel was asked who was responsible for planning and initiating the attack.

"The intellectual author of this revolution is José Martí," Fidel told them, "the author of our independence."

The people were ignited. As the second day of the trial came to an end, the public's support for Fidel was so obvious that the regimental chief realized that he would have to prevent Fidel from appearing at the third hearing—scheduled for September 25th—or risk a full-scale revolt. Even imprisonment was not defeating this rebel's spirit, but perhaps if he could just be kept off the television for a few days, the public would settle down. The regimental chief claimed that Fidel was sick and unable to appear in court, and he missed the third hearing entirely, his trial being delayed for several weeks.

Fidel used the time wisely. He had been detained now for about two months, and he had not spent his time in prison bemoaning his unhappy fate, even though he was held in complete solitary confinement with no way of communicating with anyone. Instead, the young lawyer, with access to no books or other resources, had been putting together his defense, scribbling pages and pages of notes from his memory of history and law. When he was finally brought into a different court again on October 16th, 1953, Fidel was ready, clutching his stack of notes. Just before he could go into the courtroom, the guards stopped him and snatched the notes out of his hands. All his weeks of work, all his hours of struggle and focus were torn away from him in the blink of an eye, and with empty hands, Fidel Castro was thrust alone into the courtroom. He had no friends in that room, no lawyer, not even the friendly face of any of his fellow rebels to glance at for reassurance, as Raul and many of the other rebels had already been sentenced to several years in prison. It was just Fidel and his empty, shaking hands.

But not even this would defeat the rebel leader. Alone and with no assistance, when he was called upon to testify, Fidel stepped forward. When he spoke, it was with thunderous calm and perfect coherence. "Never has a lawyer had to practice his profession under such difficult conditions," he said. "Never has such a number of overwhelming irregularities been committed against an accused man." He took a deep breath, and the silence in the courtroom was absolute as they waited for Fidel to ask for his notes back, to try to delay the trial, to fumble for words, to fail.

But he did none of these things. Instead, he continued. "In this case, counsel and defendant are one and the same." And then he was off, reciting his notes from memory. He started with defending his decision to represent himself, denying any claim of vanity, and stating that the corrupt system had forced him to do so. He spoke about the previous two hearings and about how he had been prevented from appearing in court on September 25th under false claims of illness—a statement designed to incense the Cuban public, who no doubt were already suspicious of foul play. Then he described the courage of the rebels in their own hearings, in which they had turned the tables on the court, following his example and attacking the regime itself instead of attempting to defend themselves. "As the trial went on, the roles were reversed: those who came to accuse found themselves accused, and the accused became the accusers! It was not the revolutionaries who were judged there; judged once and forever was a man named Batista!"

Then he turned from the subject of the trials to the subject of Cuba itself. He exhorted the people—addressing the public who were watching every moment on television more than the court itself—to listen closely if they cared for his country. Fidel was well aware that his trial could only end in prison; instead of trying to avoid his sentence, he used his defense as his first public address to a people that he would someday rule. It was not a trial. It was a speech, and it spoke of the courageous fighters who had gained Cuba's independence in the first place. It spoke of his revolutionary ideals, of how he wanted to change the country for the better, how he was going to bring education to the lowly farm worker and improve fairness and freedom for all Cubans. He talked at length about the economy and how it could be improved. He recited poetry, he invoked the names of heroes to whom the people had always clung. He hardly spoke of the 26th of July attack at all, except simply to state that his right to rebellion stood. But Fidel knew he was going to prison. His aim was to stir up the revolution, not to escape the inevitable, no matter how much he dreaded life behind bars and being under the control of guards employed by his enemies.

This was made clear by the stirring words he used to finish his speech. "I know that imprisonment will be harder for me than it has ever been for anyone, filled with cowardly threats and hideous cruelty. But I do not fear prison," he announced proudly, "as I do not fear the fury of the miserable tyrant who took the lives of seventy of my comrades. Condemn me. It does not matter. History will absolve me."

Fidel's speech was a resounding success, but not in defending him against his sentence; like Raul, he was sent to the Isle of Pines to serve a fifteen-year sentence in the Model Prison. But the speech did succeed in inspiring his people, in putting the name of Fidel Castro on every set of lips in Cuba, in capturing the public imagination and giving them hope for revolution. It would be years before Fidel would become Cuba's leader, but he had already become their hero. The restless, discontented people had found a leader for the unhappiness they found within them, and that leader was a twenty-seven-year-old lawyer who was sentenced to stay in prison until he was a middle-aged man.

Fidel was imprisoned in the hospital wing of the Model Prison, which was relatively modern and comfortable—perhaps a gesture by Batista to avoid angering the masses. Still, it was anything but pleasant.

Fidel and twenty-five comrades were able to stay together. He also started a kind of school in order to help his illiterate fellow prisoners learn to read and write, exhibiting his passion for educating the common man. But when the group unwisely began to sing songs that deprecated Batista, Fidel was taken off to solitary confinement, unable to speak to his friends. Instead, he turned to writing letters to his wife, to his friends, to his comrades, to everyone that he could think of. His wife, Mirta Díaz-Balart, would not receive letters for very long. A fellow UH student from a rich family, Mirta had just found employment for the very government against which Fidel strove with such determination. Fidel considered her acceptance of the job to be a disgusting insult, and they both filed for divorce while Fidel was still in prison.

It was in his time in prison that Fidel really began to put the revolution together. He named his group the 26th of July Movement (commonly abbreviated as MR-26-7), and despite the bars that held him, Fidel wasn't done with the revolution. Batista was going to fall—he just didn't know it yet. "We still have strength to die and fists to fight," he wrote to a friend in December 1953, only a few months into his sentence. "From all of us, we send you a strong embrace."

As Fidel and Raul were patiently awaiting the end of their sentences, in Argentina, young Ernesto Guevara graduated as a medical doctor from Buenos Aires University in 1953. A life of luxury was at his fingertips, but instead of opening a practice, Ernesto was determined to help the poor. He could not forget the hopelessness in the eyes of the people he had seen on his motorcycle tours and he had to do something about it. He began to travel throughout Latin America, working in the most impoverished communities as a doctor, finally ending up in Guatemala where a revolutionary had just installed a new government two years before. Here, Ernesto became involved in revolutionary actions, falling deeper and deeper into the rabbit hole of Marxism. When the revolutionary government was toppled by the CIA, Ernesto got involved in the violent attempts the revolutionaries made to take back the country, but they were all in vain. He left Guatemala a wiser man, seasoned by defeat, but nonetheless determined to bring freedom and peace—which, to him, meant communism—to the Latin American people that he so loved. Apart from experience, he gained one more thing during his time in Guatemala: a nickname that would stick with him for the rest of his life. He became Chè Guevara, a name that would soon be on the lips of the world. The nickname came from a kind of catch-all Spanish interjection that could mean either "hey!" or "guy," depending on its context; Chè earned the nickname from his repetitive use of the word.

Back in Cuba, it seemed as though Batista was aware he had gone too far and angered his people too much. He began to take steps to appease the people, starting with holding "elections" in 1954. No opponents dared stand against him, however, and it was widely considered that the so-called elections were fraudulent. Batista had hoped that by pretending to win fair elections he would gain some favor back from his people, but instead, they only grew more suspicious of him.

Seeing that his ploy hadn't worked, he tried a grander gesture. In 1955, as part of an amnesty releasing all political prisoners, Batista set all the members of MR-26-7 free.

Chapter 7 – A Fateful Meeting

Blinking in the sudden sunlight, Fidel Castro was led out of the Model Prison and walked outside as a free man for the first time in almost two years. Alongside Raul and other members of MR-26-7, he had just been released from prison under Batista's amnesty following protests by the people. He was free to go where he would, to practice law, even to speak to the people via radio and conferences. Some may have expected him to have learned his lesson and lead a quiet, peaceful life somewhere; after all, being a lawyer, Fidel had the potential to become one of Havana's privileged middle class. Like so many others, he could have just turned a blind eye to the ailing thousands that were suffering and dying in the eastern provinces. He could have just turned his back on the people that were being slaughtered on the streets. He could just walk away from it all and into a life of privilege, enjoying those same comforts that his enemies were still lapping up from their luxurious perches.

Perhaps the thought even occurred to him. Perhaps, as he stepped out into freedom again for the first time, Fidel Castro thought about leaving history to itself and becoming another member of the faceless, voiceless, heartless hundreds that just didn't care about the poor. If he had, history would have looked very different.

But he didn't. Instead, with Raul in tow, Fidel jumped straight back into the world of politics. He started to address the people again, even though Batista was closely monitoring him. He spoke on the radio and with the press, but his newfound freedom turned out to be short-lived. At every turn, Batista was attempting to curtail Fidel's activities, to suppress his revolutionary spirit. Surely spending two years in prison was enough of a lesson to dissuade him from stirring up even more trouble? But Fidel was a cockroach that wouldn't be crushed, and the more he spoke to the people, the more they loved him.

Meanwhile, Chè had a target on his back, placed there by the new government of Guatemala. He was forced to hide in the Argentinian Embassy, and much as his nature rebelled against the idea of giving up, Chè knew that the short-lived revolution was over in Guatemala. The CIA was just too strong, striking invisibly right within the organization. Getting himself killed here was not going to help any of the Latin Americans he cared about, and there was only one option left for him: escape. The embassy arranged safe passage out of the country for him, and Chè opted to flee to Mexico City.

Back in Cuba, Batista was running out of options when the riled-up people began to demonstrate more and more violently. The Batista regime grew more and more paranoid; young people were all universally classed as a threat to the government and repressed, sometimes with terrible violence. By this time, Batista was in his fifties, and he was determined not to lose his grip on the island he had fought so hard for. His measures became more and more drastic, including closing the University of Havana—a move that barely impacted the economy considering that unemployment had reached the point where university graduates could not find work anyway. The people grew unhappier with this state of affairs, and small strikes and riots broke out all over Cuba.

Finally, in late 1955, the protests became violent to the point of bombings, and Fidel knew that even though he wasn't directly behind the violence, he would be implicated for it. He still planned to start a revolution, but his followers were only a scattered and fearful handful fresh out of prison. They needed to get out of Cuba, to go somewhere safe to regroup, train, and arm themselves for the revolt that Fidel knew was the only way to ever overthrow Batista once and for all. As Batista's brutal police hunted through the streets of Havana for Fidel and his friends, they fled, escaping to Mexico. Before he left, Fidel did send a message to the press, promising that the fight was not over. If he returned, he promised it would be "with tyranny beheaded at our feet."

The Mexico of the 1950s was a country that had just recovered from decades of civil war and revolution. The Mexicans had achieved what Fidel was still only dreaming of; their peasants had risen up for their rights, overthrown their conservative government, and fought a long and hard revolution that ended with freedom. It was now a fairly stable country with a steady government and relative peace, and Fidel felt it was the perfect place to put together his dreams for giving Cuba the same things. He and Raul, along with a few supporters, took up residence in Mexico City.

Life in the city was not easy for the Castro brothers. Money was scarce, and everything they had was poured into funding weapons and other resources for the revolution that Fidel was still determined to start. Eventually, Fidel scraped together enough money to go on a tour of the United States, notably Miami, Philadelphia, and New York. He didn't bother to speak to Americans—not much of a surprise considering that the Batista regime and the United States were as thick as thieves—but instead went to the Cubans who had fled the island for greener pastures when the Batista administration had gotten too brutal for them. They were eager to help, but they had almost nothing to give. Fidel almost felt guilty accepting the tiny donations they were able to give him. He may have returned to Mexico City with only about a thousand dollars, but he now held the heartfelt support of his fellow Cubans living in the U. S.

Back in Mexico City, Raul told Fidel that he wanted to introduce him to a friend he'd made. He was an Argentine, Raul told his older brother, but he had the same revolutionary heart that Fidel did—and he was a doctor. Knowing that medical support could be invaluable, Fidel agreed to meet with Raul's friend, although he was a little reluctant to involve some foreigner with their tight-knit Cuban band.

One evening in July 1955, Raul brought his friend over to Fidel. The two men regarded one another for a moment. This friend of Raul's looked terribly young to Fidel; he wore his hair a little long, the wavy curls framing a charismatic, handsome face that was pinched by illness and poverty. But something in his eyes captured Fidel at once. He had pitch-dark eyes, but they gleamed with emotion and intelligence, burning with a strange intensity that he had never seen before. The intense expression in those eyes would one day captivate an entire culture, become a symbol of a whole century. For now, they caught Fidel's attention, and he immediately felt that he'd met a man with whom he was going to change the world.

Fidel introduced himself. Raul's friend extended his hand and smiled, an expression that charmingly lit up those dark eyes. "Ernesto Guevara," he said. "But my friends call me Chè."

When Fidel first met Chè, his initial "click" with the young Argentine was quickly pushed aside by a host of concerns. After years of living fairly roughly in the chaos of revolutions and the depths of poverty, Chè was not only poor himself, but his asthma was plaguing him terribly. He was a skinny, sickly young person, and—crucially—he wasn't Cuban. But the fire in his eyes convinced Fidel to introduce him to the other members of MR-26-7. Like Fidel, the other Cubans were immediately impressed by Chè, but they were less impressed when Fidel started giving him more and more crucial responsibilities—and authority—in planning the revolution. At first, the men were reluctant to obey Chè's orders and even questioned why an outsider like him should be given such an important role in the movement. But Chè worked hard to prove himself, and his genuine fervor for the cause and passion for change soon won them over.

Chè's fervor would also occasionally prove to be a liability at times. When authorities in Mexico happened to stumble across MR-26-7's growing stock of weapons, Chè and Fidel were arrested. Instead of making any effort at secrecy, Chè, to Fidel's great annoyance, flew into a rage both at the police officers and later in the courtroom. In a move that was similar to Fidel's "History Will Absolve Me" speech, but appallingly less successful, Chè vehemently defended his ideals and delivered a long lecture on his political views, which were profoundly Marxist-Leninist by this time. Chè's fighting spirit landed them both in jail for several weeks.

Still, their new friendship emerged from prison unscathed, and within a few months, Chè and Fidel were swimming the Rio Grande into Texas to visit another exiled Cuban who they felt would be able to help them in their struggle against Batista: ex-president Carlos Prío Socarrás. Despite the fact that Prío's regime had been almost as corrupt as Batista's, he at least was a mutual enemy of Cuba's current dictator, and Fidel knew that the revolution was desperate for money if it was to have any chance of success. Much as he disliked the idea of accepting cash that had essentially been stolen from the people he was trying to help, he knew it was the only way. Prío agreed to help, and Fidel returned to his gang of men with a donation that was big enough to start the next phase of preparations: procuring a suitable vessel to take them back home to Cuba.

Back on the island itself, Batista's measures to crush his increasingly resistant people were becoming more and more drastic. The University of Havana had long since been closed in an attempt to stifle any revolutionary activities that could be attempted by the student body; an attempt at a revolt, led by the Cuban army's general and known as the Conspiracy of the Pure, had been betrayed and destroyed; young men were being arrested, tortured, and killed by the police, often without reason. As gangsters and film stars continued to party their nights away in the luxury of Havana, the Cuban people continued to be killed and struck down any time they dared to raise their voices against the monster that unwanted little

Rubén Zaldívar had grown into. Batista was used to power now, used to spoiling himself with all of Havana's treasures, and used to crushing any opponent that dared rise against him. All of Cuba feared him, and they had reason to. It's estimated that during his time in power, Batista's administration was responsible for the deaths of 20,000 Cubans.

But this shocking number would soon be curtailed. Batista's days of pillaging his country and destroying his people were numbered. Fidel and his band of rebels were in the final stages of planning their revolution: most crucially, they had purchased a yacht. Her name was *Granma*, and she had once been a bomb target boat in the United States Navy. Although she was only sixty feet long, *Granma* immediately captured Fidel's attention when he happened to see her. At the time, she was owned by Antonio Del Conde, a gun shop owner who also dealt in less legal items. Fidel had approached Conde shortly after arriving in Mexico, desperate for help, and his charisma and sincerity had immediately attracted Conde's attention. Conde became instrumental in building Fidel's little army. He helped to keep them hidden from Mexican authorities, helped to get them training and food, and was in the ideal position to furnish them with guns.

The *Granma*, however, was not originally part of the deal. Conde had spotted her half-destroyed on the edge of the Tuxpán River, and he had thought that even in her semi-wrecked state there was something beautiful about her. Something noble, even. He approached her owners, who had no use for her, and easily bought her for the sum of $20,000. There's something a little poetic in the fact that that's one dollar for every person that died at Batista's cruel hands.

Conde decided to keep *Granma* for himself, planning on fixing her up and cruising around on her for fun. But when Fidel happened to see her, it was as if she spoke to him on an even deeper level than she'd spoken to Conde. "If you fix this boat," he told Conde, "then on this boat I will return to Cuba."

Conde was horrified. For a start, *Granma* was in a horrifying condition; practically everything on her needed to be replaced. But Fidel would not be dissuaded. On November 25th, 1956, he loaded those of his troops that were able to fit into the belly of the little yacht and set sail for Cuba's eastern shore.

Granma and her crew had undergone an extensive overhaul in the past months. Fidel's discouraged little band of hopefuls, fresh out of prison, had been drilled into an army that he believed could beat the best of Batista's forces. *Granma* herself had extensive work done to her, including the replacement of her keel and the installation of new engines. She was, however, still a craft almost entirely unsuited to what Fidel wanted to achieve with her.

For a start, *Granma* was designed to accommodate twelve people. By the time Fidel had finished cramming everyone he wanted to bring onto the yacht, she contained eighty-two revolutionaries and five days' worth of fuel—the bare minimum to get the *Granma* from Mexico to Cuba in perfect weather and with perfect navigation. Both of these decisions were a mistake. The *Granma* was about to embark on a voyage that was supposedly doomed to failure and shipwreck, but a voyage that would, nonetheless, change the history of the world.

Chapter 8 – The Voyage of the *Granma*

Norberto Collado Abreu had survived some crazy stuff in his lifetime. Having joined the navy in 1941, Collado had worked on submarine chasers in the Second World War. He was the black son of a poor fisherman, yet it quickly became evident that Collado had a special knack for working with ships. Most particularly, he never got seasick, and he had an incredible ability to work with sonar. His hearing was so refined that navy doctors tested it and discovered that he could even hear pitches that were usually inaudible to the human ear. In the navy, this meant just one thing: Collado was the perfect candidate to man the sonar machines that were used to detect the infamous German U-boats below the surface. He was sent to work on a submarine chaser named CS-13 off the coast of Cuba, and it was his amazing ear that led to the discovery and sinking of German submarine U-176—the only U-boat ever sunk by Cuban forces during WWII—in 1943.

For a brief while, after the war ended and the information about U-176 was made public, Collado was a hero of the Cuban nation. But his fame would not last long. Also disgusted by the corruption of the Batista regime, Collado found himself imprisoned for his left-wing political stance. After surviving hours of the most horrific torture at the hands of Batista's brutal police force, he was sent to the Model Prison on the Isle of Pines, where he met a man that immediately inspired and captivated him: Fidel Castro. Collado quickly became a member of MR-26-7, and when he and Fidel were released, it seemed the natural thing to follow Fidel to Mexico.

Now though, despite all that he had survived, Collado feared for his life. He had never experienced conditions as horrendous as those on the *Granma*. She had set sail on November 25th, 1956, and only minutes into the voyage, Collado worried that the little yacht and her foolhardy crew were doomed. The storm that had provided them with the necessary cover to slip out of Tuxpán under the noses of Mexican authorities was now threatening to sink them and destroy all hope of revolution. The *Granma* was being thrown mercilessly from wave to wave, tossed about on the turbulent waters like a toy in the hands of some cruel giant. Collado wrestled to keep the yacht on course as she climbed the tossing waves, a tiny speck of white in the vastness of the dark and angry ocean. Some of the revolutionaries wanted to go back. But Fidel's jaw was set; Chè's eyes were ablaze with determination. Tiny as the *Granma* was and as furiously as she was being pounded by the storm waves, she was the only hope that Cuba had. Fidel knew that their army was as tiny compared to Batista's as the *Granma* was compared to the storm. He also knew that just as the *Granma* would have to press on if they were to get to Cuba, so the revolution would have to struggle forward despite all the opposition it faced if it was going to succeed and liberate the people from Batista's iron grip.

So, they plowed on over wave after wave with sickening repetition. The *Granma* climbed valiantly, the wave bucking beneath her, to the crest of another wave; there, illuminated by flashing lightning and surrounded by blowing spray, she would hover for a terrible moment before crashing down into the trough of the wave to meet the water with a bone-rattling impact that threatened to tear the tiny yacht apart. Collado, struggling to control the helm, struggling to find any kind of a course despite his skill and experience, felt as though the yacht could not handle the pounding she was taking. Surely one of those terrible crashes would simply tear her clean apart and leave them clinging to wreckage in the merciless sea.

But the *Granma* didn't tear apart. She kept going, wave after wave, mile after mile, struggling by beneath her newly replaced keel. Her passengers were crammed into her belly like sardines, covered with one another's vomit as seasickness overwhelmed them one by one. And in fact, it was the sheer weight of the *Granma's* excessive cargo that likely was their salvation during that storm. The weight on her keel kept her stable; if she had been carrying the twelve people she was supposed to, she would likely have capsized and the Cuban Revolution ended before it truly began.

The storm lasted for three horrific days. Conditions in her hold were practically unbearable, the stench of almost eighty men crammed shoulder-to-shoulder inside and having nowhere to defecate or vomit lying thick in the air. Conditions on the deck were hardly any better, with waves crashing down across the deck, splashing and tugging at Collado's legs as he clung to the wheel. But Collado hung on, and he hung on almost perfectly. There was no way that the *Granma* could have ever made it to Cuba if she wandered even slightly from her course, something that was almost guaranteed to happen with any human helmsman. Collado, however, was no ordinary helmsman. He kept her straight and true, and they pressed on toward Cuba despite the fact that the overladen yacht was already running dangerously low on fuel.

When the storm broke, things improved somewhat. There was hardly any food on board—there was no space for food, considering there was hardly enough space for the men and the fuel. All they had was oranges, but it would have to do. Efforts were made to clean up the men somewhat with buckets of seawater. Spirits lifted, but the danger was not over yet. Now they were approaching enemy airspace, and Batista had gotten wind of what was going on. His air force had been told to look out for a lone motor yacht somewhere in the 1,200 miles between Mexico and Cuba, and their planes were circling, searching for the *Granma*.

The planes didn't find her. But disaster did. In the last night of the voyage, as the *Granma* lumbered through the waves, the rhythmic thrum of her engines was drowned out by a garbled scream and a splash. The navigator had fallen overboard. Fidel immediately shouted at Collado to turn the yacht back, demanding the searchlight to be switched on. Some of the revolutionaries protested. Switching the light on would make them a beacon for Batista's warplanes; turning back, when they already had barely enough fuel to make it to Cuba, would be a death sentence. But Fidel knew all of these things and he was still not going to leave one of his men behind to drown alone in the wide ocean. He ordered the *Granma* to turn back, and Collado spun the wheel. The searchlight skimmed across the water, illuminating only the ripple of waves. Silence fell on the deck as the rebels desperately scanned the area, searching for—there! A panicking face and a pair of waving arms. The navigator was dragged back aboard, and the voyage continued.

The rebels had to take a detour toward the Cayman Islands to avoid detection before swinging straight toward the east coast and Fidel's destination. He had chosen exactly the same spot as José Martí had almost a century ago, not merely for its symbolic value, but also for its strategic importance. But as the dawn light of December 2nd, 1956, began to pierce the eastern sky on the *Granma's* stern, Fidel, Chè, and Collado squinted at the dark line on the horizon that was Cuba's coast with increasing trepidation. This was not where they were supposed to be landing. This was not where they were supposed to meet with their allies on the island. Their charts had been wrong, even though Collado's navigation had been perfect; they were going the wrong way. Desperately, Fidel and the others consulted with Collado, trying to figure out if they could still make it to their landing spot. Collado shook his head. The *Granma* was running on fumes; it would be a miracle if they made it to the Cuban coastline at all. Chè also pointed up at the brightening sky. The moment day broke, Batista's planes would be up there looking for them, and the *Granma* was a little white target in a great blue ocean. Their only hope was to land as soon as possible.

Reluctantly, Fidel agreed. Collado pushed the yacht to full throttle, and coughing on her last few drops of fuel, the *Granma* plunged bravely forward. Dawn was just breaking as they reached the mangroves, and already they could hear the hum of enemy planes in the sky. With a splintering crash, the *Granma* did not so much land as run herself aground in the mangrove forest on this unknown area of the coastline. She came to a halt half on the sand, half in the mangroves, and all but destroyed.

The men were just happy to see land. They lowered a little dinghy in to carry their weaponry to shore; the dinghy sank like a rock, and so the men leaped into chest-deep water themselves, holding their weapons up over their heads, and waded to shore as warplanes roared in the sky. Fidel and Chè were urging them on, shouting words of encouragement as they themselves struggled through the murky water.

They had landed at Playa Las Colodaras, in the Oriente Province where both Fidel and Batista had grown up. But there was no time for nostalgia. Fidel was focused on survival. He had eighty-two men to get to safety; the small army that was meant to meet them was waiting patiently at their original intended destination, and they had no way of contacting them. They had to get to safety to set up their communications—and fast. Batista's army was searching for them, and with every minute that ticked by, they were getting closer to finding Fidel and his men. Fidel decided to take his men to the Sierra Maestra, a mountain range a few miles inland. Its thick jungle and harsh terrain would provide them with somewhere to hide from both the planes and vehicles on the ground, giving them time to contact their allies on the island and restart the revolution.

Only hours after landing, when the rebels had barely started to catch their breaths after their arduous journey, a terrible crack shattered the silence of the beach. Batista had found them. One of his patrol boats was firing on them from the beach. Bullets ripped into the poor, brave *Granma*, tearing holes in her stern where she rested on the broken mangroves. It was time to go, and Fidel hurried his men farther inland, leading them in a desperate retreat toward the mountains. If they could just reach the mountains, they might make it.

They didn't. At least, three-quarters of them didn't. On December 5th, three days into their trek, as they fought their way through the jungles of the foothills of the Sierra Maestra, one of Batista's forces surprised them. In the late afternoon, the rebels had been resting among some sugarcane when planes began to dive from the sky, showering the plantation with bullets. Earth and ripped sugarcane sprayed into the air as ground troops rushed in to attack Fidel's tiny army. Taken by surprise and utterly unprepared, Fidel's troops were torn apart by the attack. Some fled; some fell. They all were scattered into the countryside, hurt, their numbers diminished—some would say, defeated.

But Fidel wasn't done. He and one of his followers, Universo Sanchez, managed to escape from the fighting and hid in the surrounding jungle. They waited for Batista's forces to leave. The bodies of some of Fidel's men lay among the blood-soaked sugarcane; other men had been taken prisoner and immediately executed; still others were shipped back to jail. One of these was Collado, the courageous navigator that had gotten *Granma* to shore. Fidel was gutted. He wanted nothing more than to rush back in and search for survivors, to gather them and regroup them into another army, but Sanchez stopped him. Sanchez hadn't given up on revolution either, but he argued that Fidel was the most important member of the army, and that his life had to be preserved. His logic was sound, although it didn't sit well with Fidel.

They were given shelter by a farmer who sympathized with their ideals. He hid and fed them, and piece by piece, the other rebels started to find their way to the farm. The process was long and agonizing, with news of each new loss striking Fidel to the heart. His little army had been all but decimated. Over the next few weeks, Fidel and his men scraped together those followers that were left. He was overjoyed to find Raul alive and well; and then, after a few days, some men carried a wounded and sickly Chè into the farmer's house. Chè had been shot in the neck, but his trembling hands still clutched his rifle, and his fevered eyes still blazed with revolutionary zeal.

There were nineteen of them in all—nineteen survivors, a tiny handful of people who had already been through so much, and yet the long fight still lay ahead. On Christmas Day, less than three weeks after the devastating attack, Fidel gave a rousing speech to his troops with as much fire and fervor as if he was addressing a nation. It ignited them. Wounded though they were, their ammunition all but spent, they were still on fire for the cause they believed in, and their leader still burned at their head like an undiminished beacon of flame. He was going to make this revolution happen if it was the last thing he did.

Fidel soon had his sights set on a new target for his offensive. Peasants in the mountains had helped to feed his fellow rebels and bring them back together, but there was one thing that they couldn't provide—ammunition. Although many of the rebels had managed to hang on to their guns, they had almost no bullets left. The group now consisted of between twenty and thirty men, and without ammunition, that number was as useless as it was tiny. With no Alfredo del Conde to furnish them with weapons, the rebels would have to turn to other ways of obtaining guns, and Fidel came up with an idea that was almost as foolhardy as the voyage of the *Granma*: They'd attack an army outpost and take all of their weapons and ammunition.

By this time, Fidel's followers were so used to his occasionally reckless ideas that they barely batted an eye at this one. The *Granma*'s voyage was not supposed to have succeeded, but it did; perhaps, so could this attack on a tiny outpost high in the mountains.

In January 1957, Fidel led his little band of guerrilla warriors toward the outpost at La Plata, near the beach. Amazingly, it worked. Batista's army was not aware that Fidel was even alive anymore; they had broadcast the news of his death to the nation, and when the soldiers were confronted with the face they thought they had buried, their bewilderment made it easy to destroy their outpost. The rebels all survived. A few of the soldiers were wounded, and Chè—who had recovered well from his own injury—treated them as well as he could.

The land-overseer of the area, Chichu Osorio, was not so lucky. He had supposedly killed one of Fidel's men and was generally cruel and harsh to the peasants that worked under him. Fidel had him executed and immediately won the hearts of the peasants in the surrounding area.

Overrunning the outpost was just the first step. Now freshly armed and with some of the peasants joining them—while sympathizers were also drumming up even more recruits in the towns—Fidel and his men started their guerrilla war in earnest. Raiding one outpost after another, they began to harass Batista's soldiers, never striking hard, always rushing in just to grab what they could and then melt away into the jungle. They were impossible to track down, and as the months slipped by, they became more and more familiar with the mountains. They grew harder to catch and more seasoned in warfare, and slowly, almost imperceptibly at first, Fidel's army began to grow and gain momentum.

Meanwhile, across the rest of the country, the people were starting to become aware that Fidel was not dead. Rumors of his army spread like yellow fever from city to city, and the people were awed that their hero was still alive. They had been inspired by "History Will Absolve Me," jubilant at his release, and waiting in hope—and, some, in despair and disappointment—for his return. When they heard that Fidel was back, they had begun to hope again, only for that hope to be dashed when Batista told them that he was dead. But he wasn't dead, and the fact that Batista had blatantly lied to them made the people even more suspicious of their dictator. Unrest increased, and Batista's cruelty increased proportionately. People were being executed and their bodies hung up on trees to rot by the roadside, growing bloated and disfigured with flies as a gory reminder to the people of Batista's power.

Yet his power was limited only to what he could control, and slowly, Cuba was slipping out of his grasp. It started in March 1957, when a courageous young student named José Antonio Echeverría led the Student Revolutionary Directorate in an attack on the Presidential Palace. Antonio was one of many students who had found themselves rudely without an education when the University of Havana was closed. However, closing the university had not had the desired effect, and the students were still gathering with political agendas. They decided to attack the problem at its heart by assassinating Batista. The plan was for Antonio to attack the National Radio Station of Cuba, taking over control and broadcasting to the nation that Batista was dead, while his allies would go to the palace and shoot Batista where he stood.

The plan almost worked, too. Antonio gained control over the radio station and delivered a speech in which he announced that Batista had been killed and elaborated on his plan and on the atrocities Batista had committed—all in only 181 seconds. His fellow students were engaged in a shootout at the Presidential Palace, but it was doomed to failure. Batista happened to go upstairs at the moment that the students attacked, and they were easily rebuffed by the guards. Antonio himself was hurrying back toward the Palace when they spotted him. The shootout was brief, and it ended with young Antonio dead on the pavement of Havana.

The attack was unsuccessful, but it was symptomatic of the lengths to which the people were willing to go in order to overthrow Batista. It also woke the United States, at last, to the depth of his cruelty. A trade embargo was placed on Cuba for the first time, although the Mafia and many U. S. businessmen continued to support Batista unabated. For many, business was business, no matter the cost to the people.

Across the island, riots and uprisings were intensifying. Rebel recruiters were moving through the towns, secretly sending more and more people to the Sierra Maestra to join Fidel's fight. Groups of people began to protest, to strike, causing chaos across Cuba. Batista tried to stop them by removing rights such as freedom of assembly and freedom of expression, but his efforts did little to abate their anger. Some uprisings, however, were suppressed at tremendous costs to those who would join the revolution; for example, when rebels captured Cienfuegos in September 1957, a hundred people were slaughtered as the government seized the city back.

Still, the role of the people across the island was tremendous in overthrowing Batista, and they were all following the beacon of hope that Fidel's little army had become. Members of MR-26-7 were present in the towns as well, and they worked to send resources and men his way.

The rebellion began to gain organization and momentum. After Eduardo Chibás' tragic suicide, that crucial turning point in Fidel's mind, the Party of the Cuban People had been taken over by his younger brother, Raul Chibás. Despite Batista's strenuous opposition, the Party of the Cuban People was still in existence, although they knew that with Batista in charge they had no hope of coming to power. Chibás recognized that the revolution was his only hope of bringing the party to power, and so in March 1957, he met with Fidel and other leaders of MR-26-7. Together, they put together the Sierra Maestra Manifesto. Like the 10th of October Manifesto and so many other manifestos before it, all documents that had served to make Cuba an independent country, the Sierra Maestra Manifesto promised land reform, fairness, democracy, improved education, and industrialization.

By July 1957, Fidel's rebel group had grown to ten times its original size after the attack in the sugarcane fields. He now had two hundred men at his command—still a diminutive number compared to the tens of thousands of Batista's men. But the more outposts they attacked, the more demoralized Batista's men were becoming in the mountains. They were serving their dictator, but at their hearts they were Cuban, and many of them were disgusted with the gross cruelty that they had witnessed. Some of them deserted and others even joined Fidel's cause, contributing valuable information and resources. Irregulars in the Oriente were also working to harass and wear down Batista's troops throughout the province, keeping them out of the Sierra Maestra and distracting them from Fidel's growing army.

Months passed with the rebels slowly gaining strength. Fidel and Chè were looking battle-worn now. The smooth, round cheeks and penciled mustache that Fidel had on his release from the Model Prison were gone. Now he wore a thick beard and a bushy mustache on his hollowed face. Chè's beard was also ragged; shaving had become a secondary concern to survival, and it earned the guerrillas their nickname of *los barbudos* ("the bearded ones"). Raul was reluctant at first, maintaining his cleanshaven appearance for a time, but when the razor blades ran out, the beards grew and became an icon of the revolution. These three became the commanders of the army, which Fidel split into three columns for improved mobility in the rough terrain.

By February 1958, the whole of the Sierra Maestra mountain range was effectively under rebel control. The rebels now had plenty of resources at their disposal and could obtain medical care, food, and even education without much effort. They had also set up a little radio station, Radio Rebelde, which they used to spread their message all over the island—even in areas that were under Batista's control. It was around this time that a general strike was called for across the entire island in support of the revolution. The strike ultimately did not materialize as had been hoped for, but the people still increased their violent demonstrations. Farms and businesses were burned down; some areas in Havana were even bombed to give violent voice to the unrest of the people. Batista tried to use the fighting to his advantage by postponing the presidential elections, grabbing at a few more years of power.

Somehow, the three hundred rebels in the mountains were tipping an entire country out of Batista's control, and he knew it. He was getting desperate. He wanted power, but he could also see that his people were becoming uncontrollable. The only way to rein them back in again would be to remove the source of their inspiration and zeal—the guerrillas in the Sierra Maestra. Fed up with struggling, Batista mobilized a force ten thousand strong in an offensive named Operation Verano. It may have seemed a little excessive to send ten thousand men to deal with three hundred, but Batista was done losing to this ridiculously tiny band of warriors. He was going to send his army and wipe those pesky rebels from the face of the earth—forever, this time.

Chapter 9 – Operation Verano and Victory

Chè Guevara at the Battle of Santa Clara

June 28th, 1958. Operation Verano began from the Estrada Palma Sugar Mill, a strategic point near the Sierra Maestra and one of the few sugar mills that was still under Batista's control. A convoy of armored cars ventured forth toward the jungle. Their aim: to find Fidel Castro's crazy handful of rebels and kill them. How hard could it be? There were only a few hundred of them, and they were outnumbered more than thirty to one. But despite those favorable odds, Batista's troops found themselves a little troubled and disheartened as they ventured forth. Some bombings had already taken place in the mountains, and they left a bitter taste in the mouths of the soldiers, because instead of bombing the rebels— nobody had any idea where they actually were—they had been asked to bomb villages and farms. The rebels *could* have been hiding there, but it was also likely that many of these people were innocent. In fact, most of them were innocent, and they died for no good reason. Many of the soldiers had grown up here in the eastern provinces, maybe even known some of the people that they were asked to murder so brutally, and already they were wondering whether they were doing the right thing by following Batista.

Up to this point, the Cuban army had been Batista's most staunch supporter. He was one of them, after all; it had been Batista that had secured better wages and living conditions for them during the Sergeants' Revolt, and the men had always trusted him implicitly. He was president now, but he had first and foremost been a military man, and the army had performed his atrocities without question. Yet the continual brutality was beginning to wear the men down. They were Cuban too, and they couldn't always see why they should be killing fellow Cubans in the name of Batista.

Still, orders were orders, and they were not yet ready to defy their president. He was still Fulgencio Batista, the sergeant who had done so much for them. So, the soldiers and their armored cars headed toward the jungle, searching for any sign of Fidel's men in the rising heat of the early spring. Unbeknownst to them, the rebels were right under their noses—but they had planned to be there. Hidden in the depths of the jungle, Chè and his troops waited for the armored cars to get within range. They had already laid out a carefully planned minefield, and their ambush was at the ready. Batista's soldiers were heading directly into a trap.

The rumble of the armored cars' engines grew nearer and nearer. Crouching in the thick foliage, the rebels clutched their guns, sweating as they waited for the soldiers to get close enough to attack. All eyes were fixed on Chè where he huddled in his hiding place. He was only thirty years old at this point, but he was a veteran of revolution by now, and the smolder in his eyes had grown more intense and focused, sharpened by years of hardship. The members of MR-26-7 had completely forgotten their initial reluctance to take orders from this Argentine. With his work leading them, healing them, and tending to their wounds, the young doctor had earned their trust and respect. They would have followed Chè anywhere, and he had told them that they could win, so they believed him.

At last, their steel flanks glinted in the dappled sunlight as the armored cars got within range. Chè gave the signal, and the men raised their rifles and opened fire. Raids on more outposts had given them all the ammunition they needed; they had bullets to spend, and they used them to blow holes in the armored cars and their drivers. Blood, dirt, and the smell of gunpowder filled the air; bullets whined as they ricocheted off the metal, and there were screams of dying men as the panicked soldiers managed to pull themselves together and return fire. It was too late. The rebels had the element of surprise, and they ran the armored cars off the road, heading them directly into the minefield. Batista's soldiers had no idea what they were getting themselves into until it was too late. The ground exploded underneath their tires; men and cars were blown to pieces, scattered into the air. By the time what was left of Batista's troops had regrouped, the rebels had simply melted away into the jungle, leaving scarcely a trace behind but for the bullet holes in the cars and the bodies of the dead soldiers scattered among the craters blown by the mines. Chè had sent his message loud and clear: The rebels were not going to be cowed by Batista, no matter how many troops he sent to crush them.

Eighty-six of Batista's soldiers were killed in that first ambush; Chè lost only three of his own men. The revolution had turned into war. Furious, Batista continued to pound the rebels with his forces, but the defeat had badly shaken his already-demoralized men, and their offensive became more and more half-hearted as the weeks and months wore on.

The second major battle of Operation Verano took place on July 11th, 1958. General Eulogio Cantillo, main commander of Batista's forces, had finally discovered Fidel's hiding place—his base in the Sierra Maestra. Surely, considering that they were so outnumbered, the rebels would be obliterated or forced to surrender if Cantillo could take their base. The first step would be to attack the tiny La Plata Village along the La Plata River, close to the place where the river mouth met the sea, which made it possible for Cantillo to launch a two-pronged attack. One of his battalions, Battalion 17, was to come from over the Sierra Maestra's foothills and attack from behind; the other, Battalion 18, would attack from the sea, coming up the river mouth to destroy the village. The plan had to be foolproof. Caught between thousands of soldiers, how could a few hundred rebels hope to survive?

Yet once again, Fidel was waiting for them. As the advancing soldiers of Battalion 18 headed toward the village, rebels appeared like ghosts from the jungle, rushing them from both sides. The soldiers were in no mood for real fighting. When they found themselves utterly surrounded by Fidel's rebels within minutes, they didn't attempt to fight back despite the fact that the rebels were vastly outnumbered; instead, they dug in, hid in their trenches, and waited for backup from Battalion 17.

But it was not to be. The other battalion was not having much better luck. Snipers, roadblocks, mines, and machine guns from the rebels had brought them grinding to a halt. Once again, the rebels were outnumbered; once again, Batista's soldiers were reluctant to engage in real warfare. They were starting to feel abandoned by their dictator, partially because of the way that the army was treating wounded men. Wounded rebels were executed where they lay, but wounded Cuban army soldiers were simply abandoned, left to bleed out slowly on the battlefield. No salary was worth that, and so the soldiers made every effort not to be wounded in the first place, even though Fidel had instructed Chè and other rebels to treat Batista's wounded and attempt to save their lives.

So, with Battalion 17's offense halted and Battalion 18 hiding in trenches, the battle slammed to a halt. Fidel, realizing his advantage, began to pressure Cantillo for surrender. At first, the commander of the battle itself, Major Jose Fernando Quevedo, strenuously refused, leaving his men to sit in trenches and wait for something to happen. But once Quevedo realized that there was no way that he was going to convince these men to get up and fight the terrifying guerrillas that seemed to appear out of nowhere, he surrendered. Quevedo had actually been one of Fidel's classmates when they were children, and he would eventually defect—as did many others of Batista's soldiers—and assist Fidel in the last few months of the revolution. By July 21st, the soldiers had surrendered; Fidel's forces took about two hundred and forty of them captive, meaning that Fidel almost had more prisoners than soldiers. He turned them over to the Red Cross, and the Cuban army had lost five hundred soldiers between those killed and those taken prisoner. Batista's troops backed off with their tails between their legs.

One final attempt was made to put an end to the revolution on July 29th, and this one almost succeeded. Battalion 17 had slowly retreated deeper into the mountains after the Battle of La Plata, and seeing an opportunity to launch another ambush, Fidel sent a detachment of soldiers under Rene Latour to deal with them. But the straggling, disorganized mass of Battalion 17 was not the only Cuban army presence in the Sierra Maestra. Cantillo had wised up to Fidel's strategy, and he had laid a trap of his own—he was going to ambush the ambushers. Battalion 17 was not the attacking force; it was just the bait. At first, Latour's forces overwhelmed the advance guard of the battalion, but their advantage did not last for long. The rest of the Cuban army forces suddenly appeared from the jungle and fell upon the rebels. At last their numbers were making themselves known, and Latour realized that his men were doomed if someone didn't take action—and fast. He called for help, and Fidel's column rushed to his aid. But Cantillo had planned for this eventuality. As Fidel desperately tried to salvage Latour's men—a move akin to the night on the *Granma* when he turned back for the navigator—more Cuban army soldiers appeared and started to attack them on the road from the Estrada Palma Sugar Mill.

Desperately, Fidel and Latour started calling for help from Chè, who was nearby. But Chè did not respond; he was engaging about 1,500 troops who had been summoned from nearby villages, trying to keep them at bay with less than a tenth of that number of men. Two days of the hardest fighting that the rebels had to endure ensued, and by the 31st of July, Fidel knew that he was risking his entire force by continuing the battle. He suggested a ceasefire, offering to even negotiate an end to the fighting entirely, and Cantillo accepted. Why exactly the general did so when he was at an advantage for the first time and could have wiped the rebels from the face of the earth remains a mystery. Perhaps he was as disillusioned as his troops, sick of bombing innocents, sick of leaving the wounded behind. Either way, he accepted, and the fighting stopped. Batista sent a representative to deal with Fidel, and as they waited for this man to journey up from Havana, the rebels began to escape. Little by little, under cover of darkness and the jungle that they knew like the back of their hands, they slipped away into the dark. As soon as his men were in the clear, Fidel abruptly withdrew his offer of negotiation and disappeared after them. On August 8th, with the ceasefire ended, Cantillo tried to attack again; but to his horror, there was no one to attack. The rebels had all gone. They had turned their defeat into something approaching a victory, as the soldiers had thought they would finally be getting a victory and instead got nothing. It was the final blow for their slumping morale, and it was the end of Operation Verano. 71 rebels died in the Battle of Las Mercedes, but their goal was achieved—the Cuban army was pushed back, and they slowly withdrew, utterly disheartened by their failure.

Fidel saw his chance. His gamble in getting his men out of danger had paid off; the government was on the defensive now, and he knew that he could beat them. The rebels' fire could destroy their numbers. In August 1958, he launched an offensive of his own. Planes from sympathizers outside of Cuba smuggled weapons into the country, and with these and the weapons they had taken from the Cuban army at La Plata, the rebels came down from the mountains in their three columns and began to systematically take the eastern provinces. Convinced that they could not defeat these ferocious guerrillas, and uncertain that they even wanted to defeat them, Batista's army melted before the heat of their zeal as they charged toward Santiago de Cuba, Bayamo, Santa Clara, and their ultimate goal, Havana.

The tide had already turned, but the first great rebel victory came after months of slow progress across the lowlands when Fidel led his column into a deadly battle at Guisa, a garrison in the Sierra Maestra. The garrison was of strategic importance because of its proximity to Bayamo, where the majority of the Cuban army troops were stationed. While attacking Bayamo itself would have been foolhardy at this stage, Fidel knew that his little army was capable of taking Guisa—and that the boldness of pulling the garrison out from under Batista's nose would not be lost on his people or on the demoralized army. On November 20th, 1958, Fidel made his move.

Every day at about 8:30 in the morning, a patrol of Cuban army soldiers would come up from Bayamo to Guisa. They were heading to Guisa just like they did every morning, totally unsuspecting of the rebel troops waiting in the shadows. Out of nowhere, Fidel and his column attacked. Taken off guard by the guerrillas, Batista's soldiers turned tail and fled back to Bayamo, calling for reinforcements. Within hours a large troop arrived from Bayamo, but Fidel was ready for them. The rebels aimed to cut Guisa off from Bayamo by closing the road, then destroying the force that was left in the garrison so that they could take it over and defend it against the army from Bayamo—and it was a plan destined for success. The rebels planted landmines along the road, trapping the men inside Guisa and preventing the force from Bayamo coming to their aid. They still tried though, lumbering up the road in gigantic tanks. The rebels simply watched and waited. It was a thirty-ton T-17 tank that struck the first mine. The explosion rocked the entire landscape, blowing the massive tank into the air; it flipped, tossed like a toy with the force of the detonation, and crashed to the ground on its roof, where it lay like an upturned bug, helpless and manned only by corpses.

The battle did not get any better for the Cuban army. Even though Fidel would later call the fight at Guisa one of the hardest battles of the entire revolution, over the next week, the rebels steadily gained an advantage. Troops were mobilized from all over the eastern provinces—the Estrada Palma Mill, Bayamo, Yara, Baire, and Manzanillo—but none of them could withstand the force of the rebels. The garrison was taken and two hundred of Batista's soldiers were killed or wounded, while only eight of Fidel's fighters died with seven wounded. It was a resounding, decisive victory for the rebels, and it turned the tide at last.

After the Battle of Guisa, there was no stopping the rebels. The Cuban army had come to the conclusion that they just couldn't be beaten. They were surrendering, defecting and deserting left and right as Fidel, Chè, and the others continued to advance over the eastern provinces. One by one, towns and whole provinces fell and came under rebel control. The people welcomed them with open arms; the soldiers offered only sporadic resistance. One of the rebel columns was all but destroyed, but Chè, Fidel, Raul, and other leaders survived and continued to push inward toward the central provinces and their ultimate destination of Havana. First the Cauto plains fell, then the Oriente, and finally, Chè led his column toward

Santa Clara. This was the capital of the Villa Clara Province and the closest the rebels had ever come to getting to Havana.

By the 31st of December, 1958, the victory was all but theirs. Chè headed for Santa Clara, confident in capturing it. After a brief battle and the derailment of an armored train, the Cuban army surrendered with very little resistance. They were done fighting against their own people in the name of a dictator who had proven brutal even to his friends in the end.

It was the last straw for Fulgencio Batista. He had no friends left; he had nationalized U. S. assets in an attempt to salvage an economy fading in the face of embargoes and war; his tourism was faltering due to the violence, causing the Mafia to invest less in Havana; and even his oldest ally, the Cuban army, had utterly failed him. He was refused asylum in the United States, that country that had been for so long his supporter. His cruelty had repulsed everyone who surrounded him, so. at three o' clock in the morning of January 1st, 1959, Batista loaded his closest friends and family into an airplane at Camp Colombia and fled for the Dominican Republic. He would never come back to Cuba again.

Ramón M. Barquín, former general of the Cuban army and the man who had attempted a coup against Batista and been jailed for his efforts in 1956 during the Conspiracy of the Pure, had remarked that the rebel's offensive was impossible, "not feasible militarily." A fellow sympathizer of the revolution responded, "Colonel, they did it because they didn't know it was impossible." Whether they didn't know or did know and simply didn't care about impossibilities, somehow the rebels had done it. Cuba was theirs.

Conclusion

Chè and Fidel shortly after their victory

https://commons.wikimedia.org/wiki/File:CheyFidel.jpg

Fidel arrived in Havana on January 7th, 1959. He had been ready for bitter warfare to the very end, to the very gates of the city where his political career had its origins, but instead his journey from Santa Clara to Havana was a victory parade. People lined the streets, chanting his name and celebrating; the city itself had been partying for a week, celebrating their freedom from Batista's iron grasp.

Fidel, Chè, and Raul were instantaneous heroes of the Cuban people. Fidel was made prime minister of Cuba, later becoming president; in total, he would maintain control over the island for forty-nine years. He became one of the key players in the history of the world, being intimately involved in the Cold War and turning Cuba from a mere plaything and center of trade—first belonging to Spain, then to the United States—into a formidable enemy and a star on the stage of world politics.

Chè spent several more years in Cuba. He was made an official Cuban national, and Fidel gave him important roles in the government, including president of the National Bank of Cuba and head of the Ministry of Industry. But Chè was a better revolutionary than he was a politician. He tried to impose his Marxist ideals on Fidel and on the island, and succeeded in helping to turn it into a socialist state, but ultimately also contributed to crippling the country financially. Chè's restless spirit also would not allow him to serve in an office for very long. In 1965, he left Cuba and began to travel again, starting with attempting to assist in a revolution in the Congo. Later, he returned to Cuba and put together another guerrilla army, hoping to achieve the same glorious victory in Bolivia as he had in Cuba.

But it was not to be. Plagued by asthma, Chè grew steadily sicker and sicker. He became emaciated, his judgment suffering due to his illness. Finally, on August 31st, 1967, Chè and a group of his men were cornered and captured by the CIA. He was summarily executed and his body tossed carelessly into a mass grave. He was only thirty-nine years old.

Fidel would rule over Cuba for longer than any other person ever had. He briskly turned the country into a socialist state, cutting ties with the U. S. and turning to the Soviet Union for allegiance and support instead. The island that had once been America's lucrative playground became a thorn in its side and even a threat to its existence during the Cold War. It was Fidel that orchestrated the building of nuclear missiles on Cuban soil during the 1970s, leading to the Cuban Missile Crisis, the closest that the Cold War ever came to erupting into borderline apocalyptic nuclear meltdown.

Fidel's long rule over the island was also not always advantageous to his own people. While he fulfilled his promises of improving education and the living conditions of the common man, the ties he cut with America proved to be a mistake. Once the Soviet Union crumbled in 1991 and Cuba was left with no friends to call upon, it sparked the most appalling famine in the history of Cuba. Known as the Cuban Special Period, this was a time when the clock was forced to turn back to subsistence farming and transport via beasts of burden because Cuba just couldn't afford food or fuel. Eventually, Fidel was forced to open tourism with the United States again in order to keep his people alive. The economy stabilized, but this was by no means Fidel's only fault. His communist module for government proved tyrannical at more than one point; he executed hundreds of Batista loyalists and their families, treated gay men cruelly by putting them into forced labor camps, and severely suppressed freedom of speech and expression. As a result, Cuba found itself cut off from the outside world for decades. Even today, very few Cubans have access to the internet.

However, despite all this, Fidel remained in power until stepping down for health reasons in 2008. The presidency was passed on to his brother Raul, who accepted the position reluctantly, calling his brother irreplaceable.

Meanwhile, Batista went into exile in Spain, where he was able to live out his years in peace and plenty. The man who had murdered 20,000 Cubans eventually died peacefully in 1973 at the age of seventy-two. His timely death spared him a far more horrific end; assassins sent from Castro's Cuba were due to kill him only two days later, but they were spared the trouble when Batista died naturally from a heart attack.

Fidel continued to make the odd public appearance during the early 2000s after Raul took over, but it was evident that the old dictator was fading fast. Finally, at the age of ninety, he died peacefully in 2016. He left behind a complicated legacy of courage, misguided ideals, stubbornness, cruelty, determination, and good intentions. Some called him a hero; others called him a villain of the highest order. But one thing was for sure—he was a most extraordinary man.

The Cuban Revolution also left its mark on Cuba forever. It provided the island's tumultuous politics with stability for the first time since it gained independence. It also made it one of the last socialist states left in the world. Currently governed by Raul's successor, President Miguel Díaz-Canel, Cuba's relationship with the United States appears to be healing due to efforts by Raul Castro and Barack Obama. However, it remains a socialist state, one of only five such countries left in the world and the only communist state in the Western Hemisphere.

Cuba has taken on a little of the personality of the man who governed it for nearly half a century. Like Fidel Castro, it remains controversial, mysterious, stubborn, and always, always, undeniably unique.

Here's another Captivating History book that you might be interested in

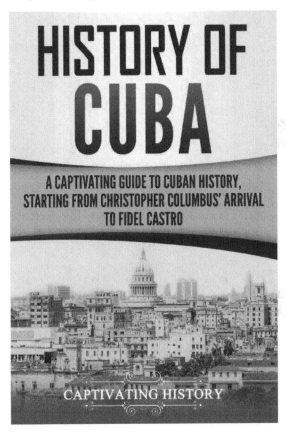

Free Bonus from Captivating History (Available for a Limited time)

Hi History Lovers!

Now you have a chance to join our exclusive history list so you can get your first history ebook for free as well as discounts and a potential to get more history books for free! Simply visit the link below to join.

Captivatinghistory.com/ebook

Also, make sure to follow us on:

Twitter: @Captivhistory

Facebook: Captivating History:@captivatinghistory

Sources

Argote-Freyre, Frank. *Fulgencio Batista: The Making of a Dictator.* Rutgers University Press, 2006.

https://en.wikipedia.org/wiki/Ciboney

https://www.blackhistorymonth.org.uk/article/section/pre-colonial-history/taino-indigenous-caribbeans/

https://www.britannica.com/topic/Taino

http://www.cubahistory.org/en/sugar-boom-a-slavery/slavery.html

http://www.tracesofthetrade.org/guides-and-materials/historical/cuba-and-the-slave-trade/

http://www.countriesquest.com/caribbean/cuba/history/spanish_rule/sugar_and_slaves.htm

https://en.wikipedia.org/wiki/Ten_Years'_War

https://en.wikipedia.org/wiki/Little_War_%28Cuba%29

https://en.wikipedia.org/wiki/Jos%C3%A9_Mart%C3%AD#Return_to_Cuba:_1895

https://www.britannica.com/event/Cuban-Independence-Movement

https://en.wikipedia.org/wiki/Little_War_%28Cuba%29

http://www.historyofcuba.com/history/race/EndSlave.htm

https://www.thoughtco.com/biography-of-jose-marti-2136381

https://www.history.com/topics/early-20th-century-us/spanish-american-war

https://www.encyclopedia.com/humanities/encyclopedias-almanacs-transcripts-and-maps/cuba-war-independence

https://www.enotes.com/homework-help/how-did-yellow-journalism-affect-spanish-american-379317

https://en.wikipedia.org/wiki/William_McKinley#Civil_War

https://en.wikipedia.org/wiki/Second_Occupation_of_Cuba

https://en.wikipedia.org/wiki/Jos%C3%A9_Miguel_G%C3%B3mez

https://en.wikipedia.org/wiki/Republic_of_Cuba_%281902%E2%80%931959%29

https://www.nps.gov/saga/learn/education/upload/african%20american%20history%20timeline.pdf

https://translatingcuba.com/the-centenary-of-the-death-of-estenoz-dimas-castellano/

https://blackpast.org/gah/partido-de-independiente-de-color-cuba-1908-1912

http://www.thecubanhistory.com/2012/05/president-alfredo-zayas/

http://www.historyofcuba.com/history/machado.htm

https://www.nytimes.com/1973/08/07/archives/batista-excuban-dictator-dies-in-spain-unending-exile-succession-of.html

https://en.wikipedia.org/wiki/Sumner_Welles

https://en.wikipedia.org/wiki/Carlos_Manuel_de_C%C3%A9spedes_y_Quesada

https://www.encyclopedia.com/humanities/encyclopedias-almanacs-transcripts-and-maps/revolution-1933

http://www.cubaheritage.org/articles.asp?artID=233

https://en.wikipedia.org/wiki/Carlos_Saladrigas_Zayas

https://en.wikipedia.org/wiki/Constitution_of_Cuba#1940_Constitution

http://www.countriesquest.com/caribbean/cuba/history/the_search_for_stability/batista's_first_regime.htm

https://www.britannica.com/biography/Carlos-Prio-Socarras

https://www.thoughtco.com/the-bogotazo-april-9-1948-2136619

https://www.telesurtv.net/english/news/Fidel-Castro-A-Revolutionary-Witness-to-Colombias-Bogotazo-20160407-0055.html

https://en.wikipedia.org/wiki/Bogotazo#The_riots

https://en.wikipedia.org/wiki/Jorge_Eli%C3%A9cer_Gait%C3%A1n

https://en.wikipedia.org/wiki/Jorge_Eli%C3%A9cer_Gait%C3%A1n

https://en.wikipedia.org/wiki/The_Motorcycle_Diaries_%28book%29

https://academicworks.cuny.edu/gc_etds/1411/

https://www.revolvy.com/page/Eduardo-Chib%C3%A1s

https://www.historytoday.com/richard-cavendish/coup-cuba

http://lanic.utexas.edu/project/castro/db/1959/19590117.html

http://www.pbs.org/wgbh/americanexperience/features/comandante-pre-castro-cuba/

https://www.peoplesworld.org/article/movement-that-changed-the-world-began-in-cuba-july-26-195/

http://www.onthisdeity.com/26th-july-1953-%E2%80%93-the-birth-of-the-26th-of-july-movement/

http://www.lahabana.com/guide/july-26-1953-attack-moncada-barracks/

https://en.wikipedia.org/wiki/Moncada_Barracks#Preparation_for_the_attack

https://www.marxists.org/history/cuba/archive/castro/1953/10/16.htm

https://en.wikipedia.org/wiki/History_Will_Absolve_Me

http://www.onthisdeity.com/26th-july-1953-%E2%80%93-the-birth-of-the-26th-of-july-movement/

http://citeseerx.ist.psu.edu/viewdoc/download?doi=10.1.1.502.1502&rep=rep1&type=pdf

https://en.wikipedia.org/wiki/History_of_Mexico#%22Revolution_to_evolution%22,_1940-70

https://www.aljazccra.com/programmes/face-to-face/2017/07/che-guevara-fidel-castro-revolutionary-friends-170711115942430.html

https://www.thoughtco.com/biography-of-ernesto-che-guevara-2136622

https://www.pri.org/stories/2012-02-24/new-fidel-castro-memoir-recalls-rebel-s-life-mexico

https://www.passagemaker.com/trawler-news/granma-yacht-changed-history

https://www.thevintagenews.com/2017/04/21/granma-yacht-the-vessel-which-brought-the-cuban-revolution-in-cuba/

https://www.thoughtco.com/cuban-revolution-the-voyage-of-granma-2136623

https://www.historytoday.com/richard-cavendish/fidel-castro%E2%80%99s-invasion-cuba

https://en.wikipedia.org/wiki/Jos%C3%A9_Antonio_Echeverr%C3%ADa

https://www.britannica.com/event/Cuban-Revolution

https://www.revolvy.com/page/Battle-of-La-Plata

https://en.wikipedia.org/wiki/Battle_of_Las_Mercedes

https://en.wikipedia.org/wiki/Operation_Verano

http://cuba1952-1959.blogspot.com/2009/12/1958-operation-verano-offensive.html

https://www.themilitant.com/2004/6815/681560.html

https://www.encyclopedia.com/people/history/cuban-history-biographies/che-guevara

Made in United States
Troutdale, OR
11/28/2023

14973012R00067